Surplus WWII
U. S. Aircraft

by William T. Larkins
Aviation Photographer and Historian

All photos by the author unless otherwise indicated

Surplus WWII U.S. Aircraft
By William T. Larkins
Aviation Photographer and Historian
All photos by the author unless otherwise indicated

Cover design by Robert Burke and James H. Farmer
Book design by Larry W. Bledsoe

Copyright © 2005 by William T. Larkins
    Copyright in U.S.A. and Canada

Published by: BAC Publishers, Inc.
                1749 W. 13th St.
                Upland, CA 91786

Printed in the United States of America

All rights reserved. No part of this work may be reproduced or transmitted in any form by any means, electronic or mechanical, including photocopying and recording, or by any information storage or retrieval system, without permission in writing from the publisher.

Library of Congress Control Number: 2005934922

First printing 2005

ISBN: 978-0-9655730-6-1

ACKNOWLEDGMENTS

The following individuals have provided information and photographs over the years and their contributions are greatly appreciated. The final work is far more complete due to their generosity.

Brian Baker, John C. Barbery, Warren Bodie, Peter M. Bowers, Charles Broadhurst, Rob Chilcoat, Logan Coombs, James Farmer, Kevin Grantham, Earl Holmquist, Robert Lawson, Gerald Liang, David Lucabaugh, Michael O'Leary, Merle Olmsted, Douglas Olson, Dave Ostrowski, Robert Parmerter, Milo Peltzer, Stan Piet, Boardman C. Reed, Stan Staples, John Szabo, Norman Taylor, Robert L. Taylor, Scott Thompson, Rick Turner and Nicholas Veronico.

Books by William T. Larkins

The Ford Story — A Pictorial History of the Ford Tri-Motor 1927-1957

U.S. Marine Corps Aircraft 1914-1959

U.S. Navy Aircraft 1921-1941

The Ford Tri-Motor 1926-1992

Battleship and Cruiser Aircraft of the United States Navy 1910-1949

Convair Twins, Airliner Tech Vol 12
Nicholas A. Veronico and William T. Larkins

Surplus WWII U.S. Aircraft

This book documents for the first time the total distribution of World War II U.S. aircraft. With over 300 photos, many of which were unpublished, it shows the continued civilian use of some of these planes as well as the scrapping and salvaging of others. It provides considerable new information on prices, totals available for sale and licensed, etc.

William T. Larkins
Aviation Photographer and Historian

The author has been photographing aircraft for more than 70 years, having started in 1934. He was the founder of the American Aviation Historical Society and editor of its journal for the first three years. He is the author of several books and numerous magazine articles. An indication of his early interest in aviation history is shown by his membership numbers - No. 1 in AAHS; 17 in the Antique Airplane Association, 201 in Air Britain; 22 in the National Ryan Club; 28 in the North American Trainers Association.

Larkins was born in Bakersfield, California in 1922 and later moved to the San Francisco Bay area. He graduated from the University of San Francisco in 1943, and then graduated from the AAF Photograph School at Lowry Field. He spent three years in aircraft recognition training including serving in HQ AAF. After the war he served three years in the Intelligence section of the AAF Reserve and three years in photography in the California Air National Guard.

He is married and has two married daughters and two grandchildren. He retired after 31 years as an administrative assistant at the University of California, Berkeley, and continues to photograph aircraft and research material for future articles and books.

Table of Contents

Acknowledgments	iii
Introduction	ix
Chapter 1: **Surplus Management**	1
Chapter 2: **U.S. Navy Operations**	39
Chapter 3: **Ontario, California**	51
Chapter 4: **Kingman, Arizona**	71
Chapter 5: **Delayed Sales**	109
Chapter 6: **Approved Type Certificates**	117
Chapter 7: **Limited Type Certificates**	127
Chapter 8: **Group 2 (Memo) Approvals**	145
Chapter 9: **Restricted and Experimental Certificates**	153

A sea of B-24s as

Appendices
1. World War II Surplus Aircraft Storage, Sales and Salvage Yards — 167
2. Storage and Sales Depots — 171
3. WAA Distribution of Aircraft Inventory — 173
4. WAA Sales and Salvage Aircraft by Type — 176
5. WAA Sales and Salvage Total by Class — 178
6. Price List for Tactical Aircraft – 1946 — 179
7. Price List for Non-Tactical Aircraft — 180
8. Transport Aircraft Prices — 181
9. Civil Aircraft Sales — 182
10. AAF Impressed Civil Aircraft Declared Surplus — 184
11. Vultee BT Aircraft For Sale — 189
12. FAA Aircraft Codes — 190
13. CAA Aircraft Totals For 1947 — 191
14. Additional CAA Aircraft Totals For 1949 — 193

Bibliography — 195
Typical WAA & RFC Ads — 206
Index — 207

The author in a frequent camera position standing on the roof of his 1932 Model B Ford at San Francisco Airport in March 1948. The National Motor Bearing Company's "Flying Seal" in the background is surplus TB-25J 45-8829.

INTRODUCTION

This is a book about aircraft that were "surplus to the needs of the service" and stored, scrapped or sold at the end of World War II. In addition to the sale of flyable aircraft to civilian buyers, it includes sales to scrap dealers to be melted down into ingots, the scrapping by military facilities, and the abandonment and destruction of aircraft overseas. Some flyable planes were sold overseas, as explained in Chapter One.

Because this subject has been such an important part of my life resulting, in part, to my wife of 55 years and the most impressive day of my life, perhaps some personal background will be useful for an understanding of how this book came about.

My interest in this subject started in 1943 when I was in the AAF and stationed at Lowry Field in Denver, Colorado. There a "junkyard" of scrapped aircraft and parts that was a graphic indication of things to come, and the sad remains of B-17B "4F," made a strong impression on me. I saw the same thing at Patterson Field in Dayton, Ohio, in 1945 when I was stationed at Wright Field. It was a fascinating place to visit, for me, and I still clearly remember seeing, photographing and getting inside the Consolidated XB-24N on a Sunday at Patterson Field. And an equal impression was created by two Fisher XP-75's — a plane that few people knew about, much less had seen. Warren Bodie was visiting while on leave from his base, and we ignored the signs and climbed the fence to shoot the rare XP-75s. The high point of that day was hiding in an abandoned guard tower when we saw a military truck approaching.

In early 1945, when I was assigned to the AAF Training Aids Division in New York City, I had a chance to see surplus aircraft for sale at Westchester County Airport. The sight of the Naval Aircraft Factory XN3N-1, Royal Navy Grumman Widgeons and the usual array of Stearmans, etc., heightened my interest in the subject. A visit to LaGuardia Field on August 9, 1945— almost a month before the end of World War II — resulted in seeing a surplus B-23 and the rare Lockheed UC-85 Orion.

In September 1945, I was given two weeks leave and flew home to Oakland. I took this opportunity to go to the San Jose WAA sales depot and photograph some surplus aircraft. There were six Navy JRC-1s, four BT-13s, three PT-19s, one PT-22, and about five Stearmans including the scarcer, at least to me, PT-17A and PT-27.

After being discharged in February 1946, I was made aware of the large War Assets collection at Ontario by fellow enthusiasts Gordon Williams and John Mitchell. They had gone there to photograph the planes, and after seeing some of the results, I was determined to do the same. So in May 1946 I took off from the San Francisco area in my 1932 Model B Ford and drove to Cal-Aero Field, now known as Chino. The managers were very kind and friendly and allowed me to drive around the field by myself for two days. This was helpful in many ways, primarily in not having to walk over a very large area, but also allowing me to stand on the roof of my car to take some photos.

The experience was so overwhelming that following that, I spent what little money I had to rent a Piper J-3 Cub and pilot at Vail Field to fly me over the area to get some aerial views. It took an hour and ten minutes to get there and back but I have always been thankful that I did this because as far as I can determine nobody else did. My interests at the time were purely that of an aircraft photo collector so I wasn't aware of their eventual historical importance. These photos are in Chapters One and Three.

On the way home I went to Gardena, Montebello, Long Beach and Vail airports and found surplus aircraft at all of them. Surplus planes were beginning to show up at many small fields and other places such as the Aero Industries Technical Institute at Oakland Airport. Their collection is described in Chapter One.

It was particularly enjoyable to watch and photograph their very clean Ford-built B-24M land at Oakland in May 1946. The reason for this goes back to my bittersweet days at Lowry Field where there were civilian guards on the gate to the flight line, and only those with a special ID pass were allowed in. I am still bitter about that 61 years later — being there for a year and never being allowed near an airplane or in a hangar. This was hard to accept after having photographed planes and being around airports since 1934. At least I had a good job as an Aircraft Recognition Instructor. There was one minor exception — I talked my way onto a flight in a B-24 one time, but it was at night so there wasn't much to see.

Although there were a few surplus planes at Oakland, it soon became apparent that the real action was over the hills at Buchanan Field in Contra Costa County, where the War Assets Administration had established a sales depot. Planes would arrive periodically so there was a lot of waiting around to see what might happen. As luck would have it there was this beautiful young lady in the office named Tillie — officially Clotilde Perez. After several months of my hanging around waiting to find out when the next planes were coming in, etc., things developed into a more personal affair. And, since Tillie knew the WAA ferry pilots, she was able to talk them into giving me a flight on December 8th, 1946 in the WAA C-47 to their sales depot at Dos Palos. From there I got a ride back to Buchanan in surplus AT-6B 41-17256 and had a chance to photograph the three AT-6s flying formation with us.

Now that the connection had been made, it escalated into a wonderful three-day trip to Ontario and back. We left Buchanan Field on December 20th in a flight of five ex-Royal Canadian Air Force Fairchild PT-26 Cornells. These were being returned to the United States and being sent to Ontario. I was flying in EW436 with an opportunity to photograph the others on the way to Santa Maria. After an overnight stay we continued on to Ontario on the 21st. The next day we all rode as passengers in the WAA C-47 from Ontario to Fresno and then Dos Palos. There the pilots were turned loose to fly a group of planes to Buchanan Field.

These were all ex-AAF pilots with lots of experience and the desire to just fly anything. There was one Grumman J2F-4 Duck there that was a prize, and a footrace took place to see who could get there first. I remember the lucky pilot climbing into it and hollering "How do you start this thing?" I was fortunate enough to get a few flight photos of it on the way back while flying in AT-6B 41-17369. Another minor story demonstrates the combination of fun and skill that these pilots shared. One of the AT-6C's did not have a tail wheel but that was no problem for that group. One of the pilots flew it to Concord (Buchanan) and landed on the grass beside the runway without any difficulty.

As a result of talking to the WAA pilots and reading aviation magazines I knew that there was a large surplus storage field at Kingman, Arizona. They encouraged me to go and so I wrote a letter to the WAA office in Los Angeles requesting permission to photograph the planes there. Their reply was that they no longer had jurisdiction over Kingman as all of the planes had been sold to the private contractor Martin Wunderlich of Jefferson City, Missouri. Because of a tight schedule I could not wait for another round of letters so decided to go anyway. After an uneventful trip in my trusty Model B Ford I arrived at the gates of the former Kingman Army Air Field on February 6, 1947.

After being escorted to the main office I was met with a round of disinterest and a litany of the reasons why they did not want anybody on their property. Today it would probably be more a matter of concern over liabilities and lawsuits, but in February 1947 it was quite obviously a different agenda. It became apparent that they did not want anyone stealing parts and items from the planes that they hoped to make a profit from by collecting and selling such things as instruments, radios and wire, etc., before the planes were melted down into metal ingots. Finally after much pleading from this poor veteran who had driven all this way in his old car just to take some photos, a compromise was reached. If I would pay the wages of a guard for the full day and agree not to leave his sight or enter any aircraft I could get in for one day.

At the time I thought this was a bad deal for which I had no choice. This was because I had no concept of the size and scope of the 5,000 planes at Kingman. I had never been there and had not yet seen it from the air. As it turned out it was a blessing in disguise, because it resulted in them providing a Jeep and driver (guard) for a full day. If I had been limited to walking distance from the office it would have resulted in my only getting about 5% of the total picture. It soon became apparent that it was impossible to see much in the distance because of so many planes, so there was no way to know what was yet to be seen.

So we arranged for me to be there at 8:00 a.m. the next day and leave at 5:00 p.m. We started promptly at 8:00 when the winter sunlight was weak, and as luck would have it, with camouflaged planes such as the P-40, P-47 and A-24 some of the exposures taken at that time are darker. The end of the day was better because it involved unpainted aluminum. One of the main problems was that I had a limited amount of film and time so it was hard to plan ahead.

It is probably difficult for today's enthusiast photographers with jackets full of 36-exposure rolls of film to understand a major difference in equipment. 35mm was almost unknown in 1946, being limited to a few expensive German cameras such as the Leica. In addition the only acceptable standard size for photo collectors at that time was 616 - a large 2-3/4 x 4-1/2 inch negative. Even the infrequent 4 x 5 negative taken by someone was cut down to 616 size for filing and printing. The problem was that 616 rolls only had eight exposures so that you had to open the camera, remove the roll, insert and format the new roll each time. This not only took time but the serrated winding knob really hurt after doing this all day.

Because we were in such a hurry to try and see everything on the field (I never did) I took some duplicate negatives of important planes in case camera movement blurred the picture even though I was shooting at 1/400th second. This cut down on the available film or I could have shot more airplanes. The final result was 352 negatives of 60 different planes — 44 rolls.

Today's viewers of the Kingman photos take a much more history minded view than I did. My intention at the time was to photograph every different model of aircraft, even down to Block Numbers, from the viewpoint of a collector. The other criteria was interesting markings, but both of these interests were subject to one general rule — no junk airplanes or planes without engines or missing rudders, etc. Unlike Ontario the majority of the planes at Kingman were in good condition and displayed a wide variety of interesting and rare squadron markings.

We started promptly at 8:00 a.m., shooting an A-24, P-40s of various kinds, P-38s, a single P-47 and a lot of P-63s. But I will never forget the dreaded lunch hour. Can you imagine sitting in the midst of five thousand airplanes with a camera in your hand and unable to do anything about it? The guard was off from 12:00 to 1:00 for lunch, so I had to sit and wait while looking at that vast field of planes. That is either total frustration or a test of endurance! But we were off again and the afternoon sun was beautiful for the B-17s and B-24s. The guard and the Jeep sort of turned into "A Staff Car at your disposal, Sir." By the end of the day we got to the A-20s, B-25s and Martin B 26s. It is interesting now to look at the negatives and see how camera shake began to creep in even at 1/400th second exposure as the time grew shorter. I was in a frenzy of activity to get as much as possible before 5:00 p.m.. And, of course, that didn't mean shooting up to 5:00 p.m., it meant driving back to the office so that the guard could check out by 5:00 p.m., a considerable difference in a field that had aircraft stretching out for five miles.

It was certainly the most memorable experience of my life and one that I do not think will ever happen again. With the change in tactics and the cost of aircraft today, we will never see 200,000 airplanes disposed of at one time again.

The next day, before leaving, I rented another

Piper J-3 Cub and pilot at the Kingman Airport. With very little money and still a long trip home I was only able to fly for 30 minutes. We started at 1,000 feet altitude for photos of the entire area and kept getting lower so the photos are from different distances. At the very end, and because we were way out on the far side of the field away from the offices, I talked the pilot down to 250 feet. That is the shot of the two rows of engineless B-17s including the all black one. The flight resulted in 16 negatives — two rolls with that time out to change film. These photos are in Chapters One and Four.

The War Assets Sales Depot at Buchanan Field closed in 1947. Tillie had moved on to become the airport manager's secretary and my connection with surplus aircraft changed to their civilian use. One of the flight schools at the field, Lightning Aero, was being run by a former P-38 pilot, a former Navy pilot and a young civilian pilot who in due course retired as a United Air Lines Captain. The GI Bill being used to provide free flight training for World War II veterans gave them the time and gasoline to fly their BT-13A. This resulted in some wonderful opportunities to get some unusual air-to-air photos. The amazing range of types that I was able to photograph in a few months include a military Grumman F6F-5, North American SNJ-6, Grumman J2F-6, Grumman TBM-3E and a Vought F4U-4; surplus civilian North American AT-6A, Vultee BT-13A, Fairchild PT-19, Fairchild PT-26, Howard GH-2, Cessna AT-17B (T-50), Ryan PT-22, Stinson AT-19 (V-77), Douglas C-47 nonsked and Bill Lear, Jr. in his Lockheed F-6G (P-38). In addition there was a Waco UPF-7, Globe Swift and an old Stinson A trimotor. I think that sets some kind of record of formation flying with a BT-13A.

The second type of surplus aircraft that I flew in was the ex-RCAF Fairchild PT-26. It was an excellent plane for air-to-air photography of slower types and I used it to shoot other PT-26s and a Cessna 140, Aeronca 7AC, Curtiss-Wright B-14B, Naval Aircraft Factory N3N-3 crop duster, Meyers OTW-160, Beech Bonanza, Larson-Holmes racer, Luscombe 8E on floats, Luscombe 11 Sedan, Stearman PT-17 and Vultee BT-15.

The third surplus type was the North American AT-6A. Because of its speed and cost of operation my photo flights in that type were limited. My photos were basically of other AT-6s and its Navy counterpart the SNJ-4.

The last surplus type that I flew in was a Stinson L-5 in February 1948 while photographing a Stearman PT-17 sprayer and N2S-3 duster.

By 1950 things had changed. Tillie and I got married, the surplus sales were gone and the planes that had been sold were for the most part repainted and assimilated into the civilian flying scene. The only large group left were the crop dusters. I had been interested in these for years so it was quite natural to continue to pursue them. Many ag operators bought BT-13s just for the engines to put in their surplus Stearman PT-17s so it was common to find many fuselages and engineless hulks laying around the small dirt fields throughout the Central Valley of California. Because ag operators at the time were very independent and resourceful there were all kinds of interesting modifications of surplus Stearman agricultural planes. This continued my interest in the subject until the early days of the airtanker fire fighting aircraft. The modification and use of the TBMs and PBYs, as well as some other surplus World War II types, is covered in Chapter Five.

My interest in the civilian use of surplus military types was, as described, extensive long before the word "warbirds" was coined. I was actively trying to keep track of all types sold and eventually was able to get copies of the CAA lists as described in Chapters Six and Seven. My goal through all of these years has been to get a photo of every type in civilian markings. It has not been possible so there are a few instances where I have had to use a photo of the type while in the military service. The most unusual one, and a real mystery, is the pre-war North American BT-9 trainer.

My first published article about this subject was a short piece *"War Album"* in the June 1947 issue of the British *"Aeroplane Spotter."* As a result of some interest in the 1970's I wrote an article about Ontario/Chino for a 1978 issue of *"Air Classics Quarterly Review,"* and a story about Kingman for a 1979 issue of *"Aerophile."* These are all covered in the Bibliography.

In 1990 I got serious about doing some

Introduction

research into the complete story of surplus aircraft. This culminated in the three-part series "War Assets" in the February-April 1992 issues of *Air Classics* magazine. This was reprinted in 1995 under the new title "*How We Destroyed WWII's Greatest Air Force!*" in the magazine *Military Surplus Warplanes*.

Finally, on February 7, 1997, Tillie and I were brought to Kingman by Michael O'Leary and *Air Classics*. The result was the article "*Return To Kingman*" in the May 1997 issue celebrating the 50th Anniversary of my first visit. The article combines photos taken there in 1947 and 1997.

So in thinking about all of this I realized "Who is better qualified to write this history than a 'Surplus Soldier' with a long term interest?"

William T. Larkins
Pleasant Hill, CA
February 2005

The author at Lowry Field in 1943

The dramatic immensity and scope of the post-war surplus aircraft disposal program is shown in this 1946 aerial photo of the 5,540 aircraft at Kingman, Arizona. (AAF)

Chapter 1

SURPLUS MANAGEMENT

The end of World War II presented problems of disposing of military equipment and real estate of such a magnitude that no nation had the experience or precedent to provide all of the answers. The United States, with the largest inventory, had been planning for the event before the end of the war based on experience in World War I. The extensive sale of Curtiss JN-4 Jennys after World War I stimulated civilian flying but also prevented the development and sales of new civil aircraft.

One part of the overall surplus dilemma was what to do with more than 200,000 aircraft. It should be remembered, however, that as impressive as this figure is, it only represents a portion of the total surplus that faced the U.S. at the end of

A similar view of a much smaller collection is this one of Ontario, California, taken on May 22, 1946. This is only a portion of Ontario's storage of 1,390 planes and shows some of the B-25s and B-26s

1

P-38s and B-24s with their engines removed lined Euclid Avenue on the West side of Cal-Aero Field at Ontario, California

B-17s stored in Germany for possible use by the Allied Occupation Force. (AAF).

the war. Aside from the non-aviation material involved, in addition to planes there were aircraft factories, buildings and airfields to dispose of in an orderly, systematic and hopefully somewhat profitable manner. And all of this had to be administered within a system that was also concerned with selling such things as 125,000 trucks, 20 million packages of cigarettes and 55 million pounds of butter, etc.

Discussion in Congress began as early as 1942 and this led to an array of government agencies such as SWPA, DPC, RFC, SPB, WAC, WAA and FLC, etc. The Surplus Property Act passed by Congress on February 15, 1944 defined policy and World War II objectives, and established the Surplus War Property Administration (SWPA). In October the Surplus Property Board (SPB) was established and W. Stuart Symington was sworn in as Surplus Property Administrator with the authority to proceed as quickly as possible with the disposal of all war surplus material in the United States.

The Surplus Property Administration tried to avoid both the dumping of surplus aircraft, regardless of price, and the wholesale scrapping of surplus aircraft, regardless of its usability. The first instance would seriously affect the success of any program to maintain a strong aviation industry and the second would be a needless waste of public property. Their official statement was:

"The program adopted provides for disposal at reasonable prices for use of surplus transports to relieve the transportation shortage, for utilization of normal trade channels, for development of foreign markets, for promotion of educational and experimental uses, and for scrapping all unusable aircraft so as to minimize the enormous cost of care and handling."

The Reconstruction Finance Corporation (RFC) took over the sale of aircraft from the Defense Plant Corporation (DPC) and continued this until the establishment of the War Assets Corporation (WAC) that was re-named War Assets Administration (WAA) in January 1946.

Part of this continuous change was the result of politics. From the beginning a venture such as this involving so much money and property was constantly under attack. Typical comments of the time are the following by Senator Carl A. Hatch (D, NM), Chairman of the Senate National Defense Committee in August 1944, "...the full white light of publicity will be thrown upon disposal of war properties to prevent skullduggery and wrongdoing, as opportunities which exist for wrongdoing, if not actual fraud, are tremendous and the temptation to profit materially will be great."

Seemingly unknown to but a few, the Defense Plant Corporation, Surplus War Aircraft Division was selling airplanes to civilians as early as 1944. This was at a time when nobody knew when World War II was going to end but some aircraft were already becoming obsolete. The WPB reported in November 1944 that 18,301 planes had become surplus and of this number 8,183 had been sold.

The majority, if not all, of these were non-combat types and many were former civilian aircraft that had been sold to the Government in early 1942. An example of this is Lockheed "Vega" 5-C NC-14236 built in 1934 and sold to the AAF in November 1942. It was designated as model UC-101 and given the AAF Serial Number 42-94148. It was used by Colonel Paul Mantz at March Field and Burbank, turned over to the DPC on June 25, 1944 and delivered to the Sales Depot at Sherman Field, Concord, California on September 1, 1944. It was sold for $5,100 and registered NC-48610. Surplus aircraft were not re-registered with their original numbers, and any 1930's era civilian plane with a number above N45,000 after World War II is almost certainly a war surplus item.

Another source of early surplus planes was the Civil Aeronautics Administration (CAA, now FAA). A number of Luscombes, Wacos, and Piper Cubs were turned over to the DPC in August 1944 for sale to civilians for $300 to $1,800 each. They did not have military serial numbers and had not been in the AAF, but they were surplus government property being disposed of through the system. The SPB reported that 6,912 of the "light civilian-type planes requisitioned for use in military training programs soon after Pearl Harbor" had been sold by January 1945. Many of these were planes that had been used in the Civilian Pilot Training Program (CPTP).

Republic P-47N remains piled on top of each other at Guam after World War II were a breeding place for mosquitoes and a health problem for the Air Force. All were in the 44-88000 serial number block. (AAF)

A collection of C-47s and other large planes on a dump at Biak in the South Pacific. Even a Northrop P-61 has been scrapped. (AAF)

CIVIL AERONAUTICS ADMINISTRATION AIRCRAFT

Non-military, but government owned, aircraft were sold as surplus including the following CAA aircraft listed in February 1946.

CAMDEN, SOUTH CAROLINA
  7 Waco UPF-7, 1 Howard DGA-18, 4 Stinson SR-8B, 7 Fairchild 24K, 3 Stinson 105, 1 Luscombe 8-A, 1 Cessna 165, 1 Harlow PJC-2.

DOS PALOS, CALIFORNIA
  1 Waco UPF-7, 4 Fairchild M-62, 1 Howard DGA-15, 1 Stinson SR-9.

FT. WORTH, TEXAS
  7 Waco UPF-7, 1 Howard DGA-18, 1 Stinson SR-8B, 1 Stinson SR-9, 3 Cessna T-50, 1 Waco AGC-8.

OKLAHOMA CITY, OKLAHOMA
  1 Howard DGA-18, 6 Fairchild M-62, 3 Stinson SR-8B, 5 Fairchild 24K, 2 Waco AGC-8, 1 Beech E-17, 1 Waco EGC.

ONTARIO, CALIFORNIA
  4 Waco UPF-7, 1 Ryan STA, 3 Howard DGA-18, 11 Fairchild M-62, 1 Howard DGA-8, 1 Howard DGA-15, 8 Stinson SR-8B, 2 Stinson SR-9, 13 Fairchild 24K, 1 Waco VKS-7, 1 Beech E-17, 1 Beech D-17.

The next batch of aircraft to be released was a group of twin-engine transports with 208 allocated by May 1945 to the established airlines. However the shortage of shop facilities and workers to convert them to airline standards, at the peak of the war, was an immediate problem. C-47's with military interiors required a great deal of modification before they could be put into airline passenger service so a decision was made not to release any more until after the defeat of Germany.

Sales continued after VE Day (May 9, 1945) but before the war was over, and an example of this was the lineup at Westchester County Airport, White Plains, New York, in August 1945. In addition to the usual Stearman PT-17s, Cessna UC-78s, and other common types, there was the one and only Naval Aircraft Factory XN3N-1 and two Grumman Widgeons from the British Royal Navy.

Typical late-war sales are shown in a July 1945 listing for Sherman Field, Concord, California with 3 PT-17s, 9 PT-22s, 6 PT-19s, 8 UC-78s and 3 BT-13s for sale. This RFC Sales Center was closed in August 1945 and the remaining planes moved to San Jose, California. Chandler Field at Fresno, California, had 7 PT-19s, 10 PT-22s, 10 PT-17s and 5 UC-78s for sale. The small Reno Sky Ranch Airport in Nevada even had 12 PT-19s and 15 PT-22s for sale.

SMALL SALES LOCATIONS

In addition to the better known large sales depots with hundreds of aircraft, the War Assets Administration utilized many small airports and operators to assist in sales. An example of this is the following list of five such small operations in January 1946.

  Becker Aircraft Sales Co., Bettis Airport, Pittsburgh, Pennsylvania. (3 BT-13A).
  Chicago-Hammond Transcontinental Airport, Lansing, Michigan. (2 BT-13A, 1 BT-13B).
  Cincinnati Aircraft Service, Lunken Airport, Cincinnati, Ohio. (1 UC-78).
  Hughes Flying Service, Capitol City Airport, Lansing, Michigan. (1 BT-13A).
  Lysdale Flying Service, Victory Airport, Minneapolis, Minnesota. (1 UC-78).

SMALL SALES AT MILITARY BASES

In addition to the small civilian sales outlets, the War Assets Administration offered for sale single or small numbers of aircraft at various military installations. The following is a sample of this in March 1946.

Beech AT-11 (41-9552) at Bush Field, Augusta, Georgia.
  Beech AT-11s (42-37275 and 42-37643) at Midland Army Air Base, Midland, Texas.

The P-40s on their noses at Walnut Ridge, Arkansas, became the symbol of post-war scrap because the photographs by the press and the AAF were widely distributed. (AAF)

Beech UC-45A (41-1874) at McClellan Army Air Field, Sacramento, California.
Douglas C-47 (41-18435) at Long Beach Army Air Base, Long Beach, California.
Grumman JRF-4 (3853) at NAS Glenview, Illinois.
Howard GH-1 (04390) at Deland Navy Base, Deland, Florida.
Noorduyn UC-64 (43-5304 and 44-70445) at Peterson Army Air Field, Colorado Springs, Colorado.

Appendix 1 lists the vast number of small RFC Sales Depots, most of which were in existence less than a year. Only a handful of these involved combat planes, the majority being established to sell Liaison and Trainer type aircraft for private use. The RFC had determined in February 1945 that "75% of the surplus aircraft on hand were hazardous for general use and not saleable."

Further examples of these small sales centers are RFC Invitations to Bids on 3 Taylorcraft L-2Ms at Dover, Delaware in September. At the same time sales were announced for fixed prices on 4 PT-13Bs, 6 PT-19As, 2 PT-19Bs, 2 PT-23As and 1 JRC-1 (Navy UC-78) at Simsbury, Connecticut. Prices varied from $875 to $2,400 except for the JRC-1. The UC-78/JRC-1 was popular and was priced at $8,500. There was constant change in the smaller sales locations, and as an example of this the following three were closed in January 1946:

Carlston Air Service, Cram Field, Davenport, Iowa; Sioux Air Service, Sioux Airport, Sioux Falls, South Dakota; and Sky Harbor, Inc., Sky Harbor Airport, Indianapolis, Indiana.

In January 1946 SPA Administrator Symington offered a disposal plane for 350 wartime-built aircraft plants. Some were sold to United Aircraft Corporation in 1947 and the Army and Navy both kept some leased plants in reserve.

This flurry of sales did not go unnoticed by the private plane manufacturers and their National Aviation Trades Association (NATA) who publically assailed the DPC for violation of the aims of the Surplus Property Act. They claimed that the sudden sale of seven thousand small aircraft was covered by the Act's policies of discouraging monopolistic practices and preserving the competitive position of small business concerns in an economy of free enterprise. The very real fear, based on the experience with the World War I Jennys, was that the post-war buyer would purchase a cheap surplus L-4 Cub rather than a brand new J-3. One of the interesting proposals made by NATA was that surplus planes be leased only and with the stipulation that the buyer replace his surplus plane with a new one "within a reasonable time." Needless to say nothing like this happened and eventually the government sold over 31,000 licensable aircraft. There were even rumors that the small plane companies were buying up surplus planes to keep them off the market.

The late 1945 sales were poor, with one of the reasons being that the majority of veterans were not yet home and in the market to buy. The first sales by RFC were in the traditional auction manner but the bids were so low that this had to be abandoned and replaced by fixed price tags. Even this did not result in more than a few hundred sales

Boeing B-17s and Consolidated B-24s lined up in one section of the area at Walnut Ridge. (AAF)

Consolidated B-32s at Walnut Ridge were less known than the ones at Kingman due to a lack of publicity and published photos. (AAF).

despite the RFC advertisements in 740 newspapers so that eventually prices were dropped and the Veterans 10% Discount was extended to a "Dealer Discount."

In May 1946 WAA announced its intention to sell 219 Cessnas in unflyable condition located in Arizona. Those with wood props were priced at $400 and those with constant speed props were for sale for $600 each. The planes were at Ryan Field, Tucson; Thunderbird Field, Phoenix; and Echeverria Field in Wickenburg. During the same month 350 Lend-Lease Stinson AT-19 Reliants, returned by the British, were offered for $1,500 to $2,500 depending upon their condition.

When the RFC set up the rules for buying surplus aircraft, veterans were given preference plus a 20% discount. This meant that non-veterans could not buy any aircraft until it had been turned down by all interested veterans buyers. The only requirement was United States citizenship. A

North American P-64, 41-19087, at Bush Field, Georgia. The Experimental Aircraft Association has 41-19085 in its museum collection. (Bernard J. Schulte)

The guillotine at Kingman in June 1947 used to chop the large planes into small pieces that could be shoved into the furnaces. (Merle Olmsted)

pilot's license was not necessary in order to buy a plane unless it was to be flown away, in which case the CAA also required a Ferry Permit to be issued.

Aircraft Sales by Bid

The WAA required sealed bids to include payment for 10% of the sales price of the aircraft as listed. After the award to the highest bidder, pay-

An early model Boeing B-17B, AC Serial No. 39-01, in the scrapyard at Lowry Field, Denver, Colorado in 1943.

The remains of a C-47 fuselage, a P-40 (39-184) from Luke Field, and several Bell P-39s sit in the scrapyard at Lowry Field in late 1943.

ment for the balance was due, and if not paid, the 10% was retained by the WAA. A lengthy disclaimer limited the liability of WAA for any sale to the purchase price.

The official description of the condition of the aircraft is interesting and is quoted as follows:

"In the sale of surplus aircraft on which bids are being invited from time to time, there will be included aircraft in all manner of condition, from aircraft which may be readily certificated and in good condition, to aircraft which are damaged and are in very poor condition or which, for other reasons, cannot be certificated. Because of the fact that no representations can be made as to condition as "flyable" or "certificatable" etc., therefore, a prospective buyer, for his own protection, should inspect any and all aircraft or lots of salvage on which he plans to submit a bid in order to determine its condition and certificatability. Such inspection should be made after the date of publication of the Invitation for Bids because the condition of the aircraft may change substantially up to that date."

Many photographs taken at this time show the national insignia either painted out or crudely marked with a hand paint brush although this was not always done. The reason for this was the government regulation as described in the following WAA notice:

"Attention is invited to the fact that an aircraft may bear insignias, emblems, or markings of the National Defense Forces of the United States or other Governmental Agency which are not approved for civilian operation, and further to sections of the Civil Air Regulations which set forth the requirements which must be met as to certification and identification marks before aircraft can be operated for other than ferrying to the base of the purchaser."

The WAA was quick to deny any liability over the condition of aircraft being sold. This was repeated in various forms and very strongly stated in the following portion of the sales brochures:

"All airplanes listed herein are to be offered for sale at their present location in their present condition due to one or more of the following reasons:

1. *Involved in ground or flight accident.*
2. *Involved in fire.*
3. *Involved in windstorms, flood and/or other weather elements.*
4. *Used for ground instruction purposes.*

The engineless B-17G, 44-83560, and cut up scrap loaded on trucks at Patterson Field, Dayton, Ohio, in February 1946.

5. Certain components or parts missing.

The condition of any aircraft listed herein may only be determined by visual inspection. Please do not telephone or write the Army Air Bases for this information."

Aircraft Registration Requirement

Surplus aircraft were sold in various conditions from almost new and flyable to scrap metal.

A registration (N Number) was only required when the plane was to be flown away from the sales site. If it was being trucked to the owners property, the Bill of Sale was sufficient and no N Number was needed.

Prior to ferrying any surplus aircraft a CAA Ferry Permit and Temporary Registration and Airworthiness Certificate was required. These could be obtained from the Agent of WAA or his authorized representative.

Aircraft Removal

The WAA had strict rules about taking posses-

The Ford-built single-tail XB-24N, 44-48753, was cut up for scrap at Patterson Field in January 1946.

11

A Fleetwings YPQ-12A (41-39055) radio-controlled drone sits in the snow at Patterson Field in December 1945.

sion of purchased aircraft within five days. The official statement was:

"Upon payment of the purchase price in full, title to the purchased aircraft will pass to the purchaser and all handling thereafter shall be at the risk and expense of the purchaser without any assistance on the part of the War Assets Administration or the Government. It is to be understood that aircraft located at an Army Air Base must be removed not later than 5 days after the successful bidder has been notified of his purchase and such removal is made a condition of all sales hereunder. Failure to remove within such specified time will be sufficient cause for War Assets Administration, or anyone on its behalf, removing the property to any adjacent or nearby location whether or not the location to which such removal is made is open or unprotected public property, all risks of damage or loss, or both, being those of the purchaser. Any expense of such removal will be at the cost of the purchaser and he will be liable therefore. All property shall be removed in its present condition and no repairs, replacement, rehabilitation or conversion shall be permitted prior to removal."

There were instances of complaints and court actions. One of the more prominent ones was the Federal Grand Jury indictment of six individuals after an FBI investigation uncovered the purchase

North American B-25J-2-NC, 43-27698, at Patterson Field on December 15, 1945. With an insignia on the nose and the camouflage paint, it was chosen by the artist for the cover of the Squadron/Signal B-25 book. The crew names under the pilot's window are 1st Lt C. A. Mood Jr., and T. T. Oliver, Crew Chief.

Another war weary plane at Patterson Field in January 1946 awaiting its turn to be scrapped. It is Douglas-built B-17G-10-DL, 42-37776, named "Lady Drew". It is marked as BK-R of the 384th Bomb Group.

of six C-47's for two Hughes companies through the veterans priority of an individual buyer.

A 20% Dealer and/or Veteran Discount was instituted on October 4, 1945, because of poor sales, and the result was a satisfactory increase. At a later date any buyer who would buy three or more planes at one time qualified as a "dealer."

Aircraft Engine Sale

The RFC had an interesting sale of 19,000 aircraft engines in November 1945. A catalog listing the manufacturer, model, condition and location was issued with a request for bids. A deposit of 10% was required and sales were on an "as is" basis with only an external inspection and check of the log books possible. Most of the engines were listed as "Used, usable without repairs."

The most interesting thing about this sale is the fact that about 80% of them were listed as "Engines On Planes" with no reference as to who was going to remove them. These were for the most part large engines that were probably only of value to scrap metal dealers. There were not even one hundred usable R-985 or R-1240 engines

One of the rare planes in storage at Patterson Field in December 1945 was this General Motors P-75A-1-GC, 44-44553. It was saved and is now at the USAF Museum at Wright Field on loan from the NASM.

The Brewster XA-32, 42-13568, was cut up at Wright Field shortly after this photo was taken on September 16, 1945.

included. But there were 3,566 Allison V-1710s!

A typical breakdown of available engines was the following for sale at Ontario: 537 Allison V-1710 (P-38, P-39, P-40), 682 P&W R-1830 (B-24D, B-24E), 186 P&W R-2800 (P-47, B-26), 84 Wright R-2600 (A-20), and 257 Wright R-1820 (A-24, B-17).

Scrap metal seemed to sell better, and in one day 167 planes were sold by the RFC at Patterson Field in Ohio for $32,000. The military was also scrapping some of their planes and making plans for extensive storage and disposition. Hundreds of B-17s and B-24s that were returned from Europe after VE Day were at temporary AAF Storage Fields such as Altus, Davis-Monthan, Garden City, Hill, Newark, Patterson, Pyote, Robbins, Rome and Syracuse, etc., and they had not been turned over to the RFC. By December 1945, for example, as many as 500 aircraft were at Patterson Field in Dayton, Ohio. Approximately 400 of these were later sent on to other AAF fields and RFC salvage depots such as Walnut Ridge, Arkansas. Some planes, such as the many B-29's at Hill Field, were scheduled for preservation and possible future use. The first batch of the 900 planes stored at Newark, New Jersey were flown out in August 1946 for delivery to National Guard and Army Reserve units.

Some surplus took a surprising twist of fate. When one thousand gliders went on sale in Pennsylvania in August 1946 it turned out that the value of the wood crates was worth more than the

St. Louis YPT-15, 40-03, at Patterson Field in February 1946. It was still in its pre-war blue fuselage with a yellow tail despite having the later star and bar national insignia.

Many non-combat light aircraft were sold surplus overseas such as this Stinson L-5 for the Aero Club of Milan in Italy. Photo in April 1956 by Giorgio Apostolo.

$20,000 glider inside. The WAA was selling them for $75.00 each, including the crates, which brought the price down to $10.75 a thousand board feet of lumber compared to up to $100 on the open market. George Driebe, of Stroudsburg, Pennsylvania, bought six in order to build guest cabins on his property along the Delaware River.

At Chanute Field in Illinois the AAF offered B-24, B-29 and B-32 fuselages for sale as homes. Buyers had to make their own arrangements to transport them to their final destination. At Fort Worth, Texas, a gas station operator used a Budd RB-1 "Connestoga" for his office. C-47 fuselages were made into temporary housing, and a company in Tennessee converted Beech AT-10 fuselages into small streamlined house trailers with two beds.

After VE Day (May 8, 1945) five thousand planes were sent back to the United States to be redeployed to the Pacific. This included 2,000 B-17's and explains why so many of them in good condition with 8th Air Force markings ended up at Kingman, Arizona. The plan was to recondition each plane and send it to the Pacific Theater, but by the time this program was under way the war ended on VJ Day (September 2, 1945) and they were diverted to storage depots.

The famous Boeing B-17D, 40-3097, named "The Swoose" at Mines Field (LAX) on May 20, 1946.

Some older planes were sold surplus before the end of the war. This Douglas B-23, 39-38, is at LaGuardia Field in New York on August 4, 1945. It became NR-56249 and later went to the Confederate Air Force as N62G.

Foreign Salvage and Sales

In March 1946 there were still some 16,000 aircraft overseas. More than 9,000 were flown back to the United States after VJ Day but much of the remainder was either salvaged or destroyed. Scrap metal was returned to the U.S. as ships ballast to conserve costs. A special AAF Disarmament Division was created in Europe to handle the salvage of over 5,000 aircraft stored in Germany and France.

The main operations in Germany were at Furth (P-47, P-51), Fritzlar (P-38, P-51), Goppingen (L-4, L-5), Hesisch-Lictenau (P-47), Holzkirchen (B-17), Kassel (P-47, P-51) and Landsburg (B-26).

Two fields in France were Beauvais, with over 1,200 gliders, and Creil, with a smaller mixture of types.

Another surplus plane at LaGuardia Field in August 1945 with an interesting history. Owned before the war by the Detroit News as NC-799W, this Lockheed "Orion" 9-D, NC-799W, became AAF UC-85, 42-62601.

Several surplus planes were used as advertising attractions such as a B-17 gas station, a BT-13 on its nose on the roof of a business and this Waco CG-4A glider on the roof of the Armstrong Tire dealer in Modesto, California.

The Office of Foreign Liquidation (OFL) offered 40 million dollars worth of saleable aircraft to the European market. Some C-47's were sold overseas by the FLC, such as 32 to the Italian government and 14 at Noumea to National Civil Aviation in New Zealand. The FLC also sold trainers, such as 25 Fairchild PT-26's to the Uruguyan government and 89 primary trainers to the Aero Club of Chile.

At the same time non-saleable combat planes of the AAF in Europe "were being demolished by grenades, pulled apart by tractors or hoisted by cranes to a sufficient height to assure their disintegration when smashed on concrete blocks below." At Kassel Sherman tanks borrowed from the Third Army were used to flatten the planes, while at Landsberg explosive charges were used to blow apart Martin B-26s. Steel cables were used to pull planes apart in Europe as well as in the Pacific.

There was criticism overseas as well as in this country at the sight of planes being destroyed. Pandit Jawaharial Nehru, was particularly incensed at what he saw happening in India and stated in May 1946, "This is sheer vandalism. I think we are at least entitled to some kind of explanation from those in authority responsible for this, whether they are British or American. In a world, and in India especially, suffering a terrible lack of consumer goods, to destroy what can be used appears almost criminal." Of course he was

Planes were given or loaned to youth groups such as this Vought-Sikorsky OS2U-3, 09396, for Air Scouts "Hellcat Squadron 7" in the park at Alameda, California, on May 18, 1947.

speaking about more than aviation surplus, but he did comment that "I saw hundreds of airplanes in various stages of destruction" at an airfield near Lucknow.

Improper storage that caused excessive corrosion and rusting of major parts led to complaints from U. S. manufacturers in 1947. Large quantities of surplus aircraft sold in India were defective and sold at prices far above a reasonable level according to spokesmen from the U.S. industry who went on to say "these ill-advised sales of defective...aircraft abroad have seriously damaged the foreign reputation and current marketing opportunities of reliable American manufacturers..."

Most war weary aircraft in the Pacific Theatre

The Consolidated RY-1, 67797, for the Air Scouts in New York in 1946. (Ed Deigan)

General Motors TBM-3E, 91622, was used as a monument by American Legion Post 158 at Flemington, New Jersey. It had the civil registration N4006A. (Frank Strnad).

were junked, creating huge scrap yards such as those on Guam, Biak, New Guinea and in the Philippines. The Navy had a cleaner option of simply pushing some overboard from aircraft carriers at sea. Flyable aircraft were sealed against the elements and crammed onto the flight decks of Escort Carriers to be returned to stateside naval air stations.

The Large RFC Fields in the U.S.

The Reconstruction Finance Corporation set up six large storage fields in late 1945. There were at Altus, Oklahoma; Augusta, Georgia; Clinton, Oklahoma; Kingman, Arizona; Ontario, California and Walnut Ridge, Arkansas. Although the primary purpose at this time was storage (the first

Vega-built B-17G-105-VE, 44-85738, at Tulare, California, in November 1965. It has gone through several changes including repairs from being hit twice by trucks veering off the highway alongside. It is now being taken care of by the American Veterans of World War II Post No. 56 in Tulare.

Vultee RA-31C-1-VN fuselage given to the Kern County Union High School Aviation Department. Photographed at Bakersfield, CA, on May 16, 1946.

planes at Kingman were put through an expensive preservation system) the RFC did start an early salvage operation at Walnut Ridge in late 1945 and this became a model demonstration for Congress and the Press. The wide publicity that Walnut Ridge received from inviting the press to visit the field, such as the photos of the rows of P-40's on their noses, resulted in the impression that this was the central and largest operation of this kind. Unfortunately the comparatively remote location, lack of publicity and visits by any enthusiasts with a camera has resulted in Clinton, Oklahoma being overlooked. If Oklahoma had been given the same publicity as Walnut Ridge it would have been seen as the major area in numbers, with over 12,000 aircraft.

It had been determined earlier that it was more expensive to dismantle a plane for parts than to melt it down for salvage. The AAF performed a test with a B-24 to determine this and found that it took 782 man-hours and the resulting 32,000 pounds of parts covered an acre of hangar space.

So a policy of salvage was authorized. After the engines, propellers, armament, instruments and radios were removed each plane was cut into small pieces that could be pushed into a large fur-

Bell P-59A-1-BE, 44-22614, at the Hancock College in Santa Maria, CA in August 1949. It is now at the March Field Museum in Riverside, CA.

Most of the surplus aircraft at Santa Maria, CA, in August 1949. From left to right are a C-46, P-47, P-59, P-63 and a B-17.

nace called a Smelter. These smelters were operated at 1,250 degrees in order to melt the aluminum but not the other metals. The aluminum was then poured into ingots, some weighing as much as 1,500 pounds.

Once the practicability of smashing and burning had been demonstrated, arrangements were made for bids to be made on a total of 20,690 aircraft at five WAA fields. The contracts were awarded in August 1946 as follows for 6-1/2 million dollars:

WALNUT RIDGE, ARKANSAS
  Texas Railway Equipment Company, Houston, TX
  $1,817,738 for 4,890 aircraft.

KINGMAN, ARIZONA
  Martin Wunderlich, Jefferson City, MO.
  $2,780,000 for 5,540 aircraft.

ONTARIO, CALIFORNIA
  Sharp and Fellows Contracting Co., Los Angeles, CA.
  $404,593 for 1,390 aircraft.

Ford-built B-24M-25-FO, 44-51556, at the Aero Industries Technical Institute at Oakland Airport, CA. It was flown in on May 2, 1946.

Curtiss-built TP-47G-10-CU, 42-25068, at Oakland on August 24, 1946. It was later sold and became N42354.

ALBUQUERQUE, NEW MEXICO
Compressed Steel Company, Denver, CO.
$411,275 for 1,540 aircraft.

CLINTON, OKLAHOMA
Sherman Machine and Iron Works, Oklahoma City, OK.
$1,168,550 for 7,600 aircraft.

The contracts allowed from 9 to 14 months to clear the fields and the aluminum scrap was to be disposed of within 14 months.

An intense dispute immediate arose at Kingman. The planes had been sold "as is" by the Los Angeles Office of the War Assets Administration. After this had been done, the Washington Office of WAA ordered the 2-1/2 to 3 million gallons of gasoline in the planes to be sold separately. After considerable discussion, reinforced by Wunderlich's statement that he was not interested in buying the planes without the gasoline, the Washington Office reversed their decision.

Although difficult to transfer and sell, this was an important factor in large purchases. When Paul Mantz and some associates bought 475 planes at Stillwater, Oklahoma, in February 1946 the remaining fuel paid for half their cost. Unfortunately, expenses were such that all but about ten were sold to scrap dealers in Oklahoma. The famous P-51C racers used by Mantz in the Bendix Race, as well as his B-25 modified to photograph Cinerama, came from this field.

Mantz had considerable national publicity over his purchase as the "largest private owner" and "owner of the largest private air force in the world" in the New York Times and subsequent wire service stories. But he was actually outdone by a Dallas oilman, H. W. Snowden, who bought 850 aircraft at Hicks Field in Fort Worth, Texas. A February 1947 photo shows him with acres of Cessna UC-78's and Vultee BT-13's.

Many smaller lots of planes were sold to individual bidders in an attempt to get rid of as many aircraft as possible as fast as possible. William Steiner of Anaheim, California, for example, bought 35 non-flyable Beech GB-1's (D-17S) for $72,856. These had been returned from England under the Lend-Lease Program and were "as is" in Richmond, Virginia. Many lots of Vultee BT-13's were sold to crop dusters for their engines. For years after the War one could see engineless BT-13 hulks in the weeds and behind hangars at small airports all over the West.

This Bell P-39Q-15-CE, 44-2738, was another plane for use in training aircraft mechanics at the Aero Industries Technical Institute at Oakland Airport.

Globe-built Beech AT-10-GF, 42-35009, at Aero Industries Tech in August 1946. The painting out of the national insignia was a requirement of surplus sales that was not always done.

The demand for Stearmans was so great that lotteries had to be held to select the buyers. This February 1947 photo shows the WAA Administrator holding a jar with 46 names for a drawing to sell three N2Ss for $400 each at Buchanan Field. WAA employee, and future Mrs. Larkins, is second from the right at the counter.

SALES OF NEW L-5G AIRCRAFT

After the war ended there were sales of new aircraft and parts. An example of this was the sale of 34 new Stinson L-5G's (AAF 45-35031 to 45-35064) at the Ford Willow Run Airport, Hangar #41, Ypsilanti, Michigan in February 1946.

In this particular case the sale was for the entire batch of aircraft and parts as a lot with no bids accepted for individual aircraft even though they were all listed by AAF serial number. The stated estimate of the original price of the lot to the AAF was $124,027. They were described as "L-5G airframes" practically complete to the firewall. A kit consisting of many of the parts forward of the firewall including a new Lycoming 0-435-11 engine was included for each airframe.

In addition, and as part of the bid lot, the following parts for the L-5G and OY-1 were included:

Air Speed Pitot Heads, Control Columns, Doors, Elevators, Flaps, Fuel Tanks, Landing Gears, Rudders, Seats, Tail wheels and Tires, Vertical Fins, Windows, Wings and Wing Struts.

TRANSPORT AIRCRAFT

By the end of 1945 the RFC had allocated transports at a set price for airline sale as a 5-year lease.

The airlines preferred the lease arrangement as their intention was to fly the planes only until new post-war types such as the Douglas DC-6 became available. 184 DC-3 types and 1760 C-54s were allocated to domestic airlines and 74 DC-3s and 44 C-54s to foreign airlines. 22 airlines were asking for 170 planes for commercial flight. In October 1945 the first C-54 was sold to Northwest Airlines. In February 1946 Air Cargo Transport Corporation, one of the first non-scheduled airlines, bought five DC-3s and two C-54s. In

This rare Stearman PT-18, 40-2014, at Sherman Field, Concord, CA on April 15, 1945 is typical of the post-war scene of many Stearmans sitting in the weeds awaiting sale by WAA. Sherman also had a variety of types for sale, including the PT-19, PT-22, UC-78, JRC-1, L-2, L-3, and the rare UC-81F and UC-101. (Earl Holmquist).

Vultee BT-13B, 42-90071, with UC-78s and PT-17s awaiting sale by WAA at Sherman Field in April 1945. The Air Transport Command insignia on the rear of the fuselage is a rare sight on a basic trainer. (Earl Holmquist)

A camouflaged Douglas B-18, 36-279, at Vail Field (Montebello), CA in May 1946. The wing and tail form show its connection to the DC-3, and like that rugged plane, it is still flying and up for sale after ten years of service.

This Howard GH-1 (09394) shows the proper removal of the national insignia and military markings prior to sale as a surplus aircraft. The unusual insignia is for NASTI - Naval Air Station Terminal Island. The photo was taken on January 9, 1947 at Concord, CA, where it was sold for $2,000.

August Universal Air Lines was the highest bidder for the seven Boeing 314A flying boats operated for the Navy by Pan American Airways during World War II.

The foreign sales were expedited by the establishment of a Latin-American Sales Center built by the AAF at the Miami Air Depot. This was a center for sales to both governments and airlines in Central and South America. [*See Appendix 8 for transport plane prices*.]

Most of the passenger configuration DC-3s that were "impressed" by the AAF from the airlines were under a different policy that planned for their return to the airlines. Thus, these various models that were not C-47s did not show up in surplus sales, and the result was that all of the veterans bidding for a DC-3 to start a new airline were limited to buying and converting C-47's. So the relatively inexpensive C-47 became the backbone of the new "nonsked" airlines, and at least 187 operators' names have been identified as using them in the immediate post-war period. Some were operated as-is with their original side-seating benches, while others were used unconverted for cargo.

Transport Plane Leases

In addition to outright sales, transport planes such as the DC-3/C-47, C-46 and C-54 were leased for five year periods to qualified applicants. This was the main source of availability to the airlines in the immediate post-war period of late 1945 and early 1946. By December 31, 1945 the AAF had declared 258 of the DC-3 type surplus with 184 allocated for domestic airline use and 74 assigned for sale to foreign airlines. In addition 285 Douglas C-54s were declared surplus, and of these, 170 were for domestic airlines and 46 for foreign airlines.

The leasing arrangement was made to expedite the disposal of surplus transports and to make them more widely available for civilian use. A clause allowed the cancellation after one year in order to buy new aircraft. The WAA changed this disposal program on July 1, 1946 because it was having a negative effect on the sales program. A later form of this existed when the USAF leased a number of C-54s for airline use.

Bell P-63C-5-BE, 44-4178, at Grand Central Air Terminal, Burbank, CA in May 1946.

Not only does this Cessna UC-78B-1-CE, 43-32277, surplus from Minter Field not have its national insignia painted out - it has two! The Vultee RA-31C is on the left. Bakersfield, CA, May 16, 1946.

Grumman J4F-2, Royal Navy "Gosling I" FP456, at Westchester County Airport, NY in August 1945. It was built as U. S. Navy 32986, assigned to Lend-Lease, returned at the end of the war and sold surplus as NC-41826 by the WAA.

Schools and Memorials

SPB Regulation 4 "Disposal of Surplus Aeronautical Property to Educational Institutions for Nonflight Use" legalized an extensive allocation of aircraft to schools for mechanics training and became the basis for further "gifts" to cities for War Memorials. Some of the planned assignments, proudly proclaimed by the WAA in 1944, were B-17's "Five Grand" for Seattle, "The Swoose" for Los Angeles, the "Memphis Belle" for Memphis, and an impressive 11 aircraft for the city of Athens, Georgia. The B-29's "City of Athens" and "City of Milwaukee" were to be assigned to those cities once they became surplus. By late 1946 the WAA had reported nearly 200 planes in this program. Sadly, many cities failed to support the preservation of these planes and the grand plan never materialized. The Williamsport Pennsylvania Technical Institute was the first school to get a surplus plane for non-flight use under the RFC education distribution program when it was delivered in June 1945.

One unique use of the School Sales Program was the purchase of a Curtiss C-46 for $200 for the Kern County, California, School District. Supervisor Peter Bancroft bought the plane for use as a classroom and hired an ex-Hump pilot for $50 (plus $20 for gas and oil) to fly it to the Weedpatch Airport. From there is was towed by truck to the school at Arvin. His explanation was simple "Where else could we buy or rent a temporary room that will seat 35 children for $270?"

Public Schools were not the only ones to benefit from this program. Hancock College in Santa Maria, California, acquired a veritable museum, as can be seen by the photo of the lineup.

Several of the planes went on to other owners at a later date, and warbird enthusiasts will be able to identify several of the following planes; P-38J 44-23314, P-47D 42-23278, P-59A 44-22614, P-63A 42-68894, B-17F 42-6073 and C-46A 42-3656.

Similarly, the Aero Industries Technical Institute at Oakland Airport, California, had TP-47G 42-25068, P-39Q 44-2738, B-24M 44-51556, AT-10 42-35009 and F4U-1 55805.

The "educational" clause was stretched even further to include Air Scout Squadrons. Alameda, California had a Vought OS2U-3; Santa Rosa, California a P-61B; and most unlikely of all was the Armonk Village, New York, squadron with a

Lockheed P-38M, 44-53082, an almost new night fighter for sale at Sherman Field in March 1946. The engines were removed for a racing boat and the plane sold to become N62805.

Howard UC-70, 42-53004, at Sherman Field, CA, in April 1945. This was actor Wallace Beery's DGA-15P, NC-28406, before the war. (John Larkins)

Noorduyn "Norseman" C-64A, 44-70370, used as a flying ambulance. Photo at Palo Alto, CA, in September 1945 after being transferred as government property to the U. S. Forest Service where it became NC-58689.

The post-war scene was filled with parts of surplus aircraft at small airports. This somewhat unusual sight was at San Carlos, CA, in September 1947. It shows the remains of Vultee BT-15, 42-41885, with the Training Field markings of R-272.

Lockheed "Vega" UC-101, 42-94148 at Sherman Field, CA, on September 10, 1944. This rare "Vega" was NC-14236 before the war and NC-48610 after being sold surplus. It was used during World War II by Col. Paul Mantz. (John Larkins)

Fairchild AT-21-FB, 42-11715, at Vail Field, CA, on May 17, 1946. The FB indicates that it was built at the Fairchild plant in North Carolina.

Columbia-built Grumman J2F-6, 32681, in excellent condition at Concord, CA, in December 1946. It became N1235N.

flyable Consolidated RY-1. This Navy version of the C-87 was sold to the North Castle Youth Council for $350 to be used as a clubhouse for educational purposes, and two volunteer pilots, R. G. Burnstrom and W. E. Byers, flew the plane from Augusta, Georgia, to White Plains, New York in December 1946. The plan was to remove the wings and tow the plane over the highways five miles to the clubhouse site.

The Navy, in true independent style, continued a long tradition of giving planes to schools. This dated back to the 1920's when several Vought UO-1a and Martin MO-1s were given to schools, and at one time in 1930 the Navy gave 16 Boeing FB-5 fighters to high schools. This continued even during the war with an example being a Curtiss SO3C being given to the Danville, California, High School in 1944. The Navy also developed their own policy on surplus disposal as explained in Chapter 2.

In November 1946 the Civil Aeronautics Board (CAB) announced a new Part 4 to the Civil Air Regulations to provide limited airworthiness standards for certain military surplus aircraft and at the same time created the "NL" registration prefix. The CAA issued the Limited Type Certificates if there was no civilian aircraft of essentially the same basic model for which an Approved Type Certificate had been issued and this is fully described and illustrated in Chapter 7.

One type that did not make the NL List was the Convair B-32. Milton J. Reynolds announced on July 9, 1947 that he had arranged that day to purchase a B-32 and that William Odom, who flew the "Reynold Bombshell" A-26 around-the-world from West to East, would be the pilot for another round the world flight across the North and South Poles in the B-32. A B-32 could be purchased for $32,500 and this would have been an impressive flight, had it taken place.

Scenic flights in a surplus R4D-1 operated by S.S.W. at Concord, CA, in 1946. This is how flights were made over Yosemite Valley and other locations. Tillie Perez (the future Mrs. Larkins) is third from the right. Pilot and flight operator Gladys Davis is on the far right. (Larkins Collection)

Curtiss-Wright Travel Air B-14B, NC-68261, at Concord in March 1947. This was formerly a CAA plane, NC-1A, and is still painted in their black and orange colors. See Eagle Field, Dos Palos, CA in Appendix 9.

Fairchild PT-26 "Cornell Mk. I," Royal Canadian Air Force FH716. It is on a used car lot near Lindbergh Field in San Diego in 1946. (Henry Arnold)

The End of the Program

By mid-1947 the War Assets Administration sales were winding down, although it continued until June 1949. Prices were slashed to get rid of large numbers of planes such as the 506 C-46's at Walnut Ridge. Depending upon condition, the price went as low as $10,000 for a flyable C-46. This made possible the large use of C-46's by the new Non-Scheduled airlines (nonskeds).

By July 1947 approximately 65,000 airplanes had been disposed of; 35,000 sold for civilian use, 10,000 sold for scrap, and the storage fields had been reduced to three. Major General Robert Littlejohn, WAA Administrator, summarized some of the problems that had been encountered as follows:

1. Poor Organization. The Office of the Administrator was expected to tackle every problem, make every decision and take every action of importance. This resulted in a deluge of 7,500 letters and from 400 to 700 phone calls per day. The 33 Regional Offices operated basically as separate empires.

2. Stock Control. The inventory was inaccurate and in many case non-existent. Records in many instances were only 20% accurate.

3. Sales Programs. None had target dates for accomplishment. The WAA was committed completely to site sales and sale by contracts, with the result that businesses quit buying and sales dropped to minimal figures.

4. Disservice to Veterans. The operation bogged down with a million and a half outstanding certificates. Certificates were issued against non-existent supplies and veterans were infuriated by inaction and brush-offs.

5. Real Property Disposal. Inaction on idle facilities and laxity in negotiations in dealings with irresponsible bidders. Airport transfers were enmeshed in red tape, requiring 12 months for clearance.

The seldom seen Douglas A-33, 42-13594, from Las Vegas AAF (now Nellis AFB), visiting Moffett Field on March 7, 1942. The placement of the AAF Serial Number on the tail is unusual. One A-33 was offered for sale at Augusta, Georgia.

Lockheed C-69, 42-94559, now NC-74192 in the beautiful red-white-blue colors of California Hawaiian Airlines. See WAA advertisement "Constellations For Sale". Photographed at Oakland Airport in February 1953.

Despite all of this some 65,000 aircraft were disposed of in about a year and a half and it should be remembered again that airplanes were only one part of the overall surplus disposal effort faced by the government.

The final sale was probably the 150 Curtiss C-46D's for the Nationalist Chinese government that were taken out of storage, reconditioned, painted and flown to Oakland, California in 1948. The contract to deliver all of these by air to Shanghai was completed without a loss by Transocean Air Lines to provide a fitting end to the World War II surplus aircraft program.

A group of C-46s for the Nationalist Chinese Air Force constituted the last batch of sales of World War II surplus aircraft in the immediate post-war period. This plane, C-46F serial number C-46289, is one of those overhauled and painted under a contract with Transocean Air Lines who also delivered them by air. Photo at Oakland, CA, on August 17, 1948.

Surplus Management

Constellations FOR SALE

HOW TO BUY

Bids may be entered only for individual aircraft. Each bid must be accompanied by a certified or cashier's check payable to The Treasurer of the United States in the amount of ten percent of the total bid price. Bids will be opened at 12 o'clock noon, March 12th, 1947, in the Office of Aircraft Disposal, Room 395, 425 Second Street, N. W., Washington, D. C.

* * *

Consult your nearest WAA Regional Office regarding method to be followed in submitting bids, terms and conditions of sale, or such other information as you may desire.

* * *

Envelopes containing bids should be plainly marked on the lower left-hand corner, "Sealed bid on Constellation Identification Number .... Opening date March 12, 1947."

* * *

Bids from veterans must show certification date, case number and location of certifying office.

* * *

Priority purchasers are not required to bid any specified amount but are invited to submit their offer to purchase any of these aircraft at their fair value. The fair value of each aircraft will be determined by an analysis of bids submitted by non-priority bidders and will be the lowest price at which each aircraft will be awarded to a non-priority bidder. All priority purchasers will immediately be notified of the fair value established on the aircraft in which they are interested and will be given forty-eight hours after such notification to submit a firm purchase order for such aircraft, together with a cashier or certified check in the amount of ten percent of such fair value. These aircraft have already been offered to Federal Agencies.

* * *

Bidders' letters should contain the following statement: "This offer is subject to War Assets Administration's standard conditions of sale, and all other advertised terms and conditions, and no other terms or conditions shall be binding on War Assets Administration."

* * *

EXPORTERS AND FOREIGN PURCHASERS: Your bid is solicited. Any inquiries regarding export control should be referred to Office of International Trade, Department of Commerce, Washington, D. C.

The War Assets Administration invites you to bid on nine grounded Lockheed "Constellations" (Army Model C-69) aircraft which have been declared surplus.

These all-purpose low-wing Heavy Transports are of all-metal construction, with dual wheel tricycle landing gear and triple vertical tail surfaces. They are powered with four Wright 2200 HP engines and equipped with Hamilton Standard three-blade propellers. Their ability to carry heavy loads at high cruising speed for long distances makes them very desirable for either cargo or passenger operation.

These aircraft are available for inspection at Lockheed Air Terminal, Burbank, California, after February 24, 1947.

NOTE: *The hours of airplane and engine operation shown were taken from records (where furnished with the airplane) and such hourly figures are for information only.*

MODEL	IDENT. NO.	MFR.	MAKE OF ENGINE	H. P.	AIRPLANE HOURS	TOTAL ENGINE HOURS	ENGINE HOURS SINCE O. H.
C-69	42-94549	Lockheed	Wright	2200	280	L-280 L-280 R-280 R-280	L-New L-New R-New R-New
C-69	42-94550	Lockheed	Wright	2200	472	L-472 L-472 R-472 R-472	L-New L-New R-New R-New
C-69	43-10310	Lockheed	Wright	2200	355	L-121 L-308 R-328 R-305	L-New L-Unk. R-New R-Unk.
C-69	43-10311	Lockheed	Wright	2200	1427	L-422 L-152 R-422 R-372	L-New L-New R-New R-New
C-69	43-10312	Lockheed	Wright	2200	1303	L-854 L-854 R-854 R-259	L-Unk. L-Unk. R-Unk. R-Unk.
C-69	43-10313	Lockheed	Wright	2200	180	L-180 L-171 R-180 R-164	L-New L-New R-New R-New
C-69	43-10314	Lockheed	Wright	2200	552	L-533 L-468 R-151 R-42	L-New L-New R-New R-New
C-69	43-10315	Lockheed	Wright	2200	44	L-43 L-5 R-43 R-43	L-43 L-5 R-43 R-43
C-69	43-10316	Lockheed	Wright	2200	90	L-112 L-90 R-90 R-90	L-New L-New R-New R-New

Office of Aircraft Disposal: 425 Second St., N.W., Washington 25, D. C.

WAR ASSETS ADMINISTRATION

Offices located at: Atlanta • Birmingham • Boston • Charlotte • Chicago • Cincinnati • Cleveland • Dallas • Denver • Detroit • Fort Worth • Helena • Houston • Jacksonville • Kansas City, Mo. • Little Rock • Los Angeles • Louisville • Minneapolis • Nashville • New Orleans • New York • Omaha • Philadelphia • Portland, Ore. • Richmond • Salt Lake City • St. Louis • San Antonio • San Francisco • Seattle • Spokane • Tulsa

RECONSTRUCTION FINANCE CORPORATION
200 Bush Street
San Francisco 4, California

July 26, 1945

Cpl. William T. Larkins
Aircraft Analyst, Recognition Section
A.A.F. Training Aids Division
One Park Avenue
New York City 16, New York
    Re: Surplus Aircraft

Dear Sir:

    This will acknowledge receipt of your correspondence dated July 16, 1945, requesting information about the sale of surplus airplanes by Reconstruction Finance Corporation.

    This Agency is now offering for disposal, subject to prior sale, the following described aircraft, which are located at the Sales Centers indicated in the tabulation:

SHERMAN FIELD - Concord, California - Supervisor: Mr. B. N. Cosner

3 Boeing PT-17 aircraft - price range $1275.00 to $1490.00
9 Ryan PT-22 aircraft - price range $1075.00 to $1740.00
6 Fairchild PT-19 aircraft - price range $1075.00 to $1990.00
8 Cessna UC-78 aircraft - priced at $8500.00 each
3 Vultee BT-13 aircraft - price range $3800.00 to $4000.00

RENO SKY RANCH - Reno, Nevada - Supervisor: Mr. G. F. Douglas

12 Fairchild PT-19 aircraft - price range $875.00 to $1490.00
15 Boeing PT-27 aircraft - price range $1075.00 to $1990.00

CHANDLER FIELD - Fresno, California - Supervisor: Mr. G. Milne

7 Fairchild PT-19 aircraft - price range $1075.00 to $1990.00
10 Ryan PT-22 aircraft - price range $1075.00 to $1990.00
10 Boeing PT-17 aircraft - price range $875.00 to $1990.00
5 Cessna UC-78 aircraft - priced at $8500.00

    Please be advised that Concord Sales Center is being discontinued approximately August 3, 1945. Therefore, all aircraft located at this Sales Center will, by that date, be moved to Pacific Air Schools, San Jose Airport, San Jose, Calif., which has been established as a new Sales Center in lieu of Sherman Field.

230

Chapter 2

U.S. Navy Operations

The Navy operated an independent system that included storage, salvage and sales, as well as sending some planes to War Assets for sale. This continued a long tradition of the Navy donating aircraft to educational institutions dating back to the 1920's with a group of early Voughts, and at one time in 1930 giving sixteen Boeing FB-5 fighters to high schools. This continued even during the war, an example being the gift of a Curtiss SO3C to the Danville, California, high school in 1944.

Earlier that year Vice Admiral D. B. Radford, heading a Board of Supply Officers, had developed a policy for post-war Navy surplus. One of the decisions was to operate a Navy salvage base and this began at NAS Jacksonville, Florida, in 1945, and while the war was still going on, used German Prisoners of War to segregate materials into usable lots. The Navy built its own smelter and this was watched closely by Reconstruction Finance Corporation executives and was used as the basis for their first operation at Walnut Ridge, Arkansas. When the war ended this was expanded to additional Navy bases.

In March 1946 the Chief of Naval Operations established an aircraft storage program for up to 6,000 aircraft that needed to be preserved and stored for future possible use. At the same time 360 "surplus" Grumman F6F "Hellcats" were converted to target drones. After the war ended large numbers of planes were put into temporary storage at various Naval Air Stations such as Alameda and San Diego.

An aerial view of NAS Clinton, Oklahoma, in 1946. This field was not only primarily Navy aircraft but it was the largest storage facility in the United States with 8,839 aircraft when they were sold as scrap metal to the Sherman Machine and Iron Works of Oklahoma City. (U. S. Navy)

The Navy designed and built guillotine at NAS Norfolk, Virginia. (U. S. Navy)

Many planes were destroyed in the Pacific by burial or dumping into the ocean, but some were returned to the United States as shown in this photo of the Escort Carrier USS Bairoko CVE-115. Aircraft on the deck from left to right are 16 F4Us, four R4Ds, four TBMs, one F6F, one F4U, three SNBs, four SB2Cs, one F4U, two OY-1s, two SNJs, one J4F-2, one J2F-6, two F4Us and one SB2C. (U. S. Navy)

Grumman F6Fs lined up at NAS Alameda in May 1947. Their compact storage due to folding wings results in a different impression than the aerial photos of Kingman or Ontario. Many of these Hellcats were saved for use by the Naval Reserve.

NAF Litchfield Park

The former Goodyear Modification Plant at Litchfield Park, Arizona, closed in early 1946 and the field was converted to a Bureau of Aeronautics storage pool for long-term storage. By the end of the year, over 300 new and newly-overhauled multi-engine planes had been preserved and stored at Naval Air Facility Litchfield Park. By mid-1948 hundreds more had been flown in, of the following types: Beech SNB and JRB, Convair PB4Y-1 and PB4Y-2, Curtiss R5C, Douglas JD (A-26), Douglas R4D, General Motors TBM, Lockheed PV-2 and North American SNJ. Sales of these aircraft to civilian buyers was done by the Navy on a Bid basis and it became the primary source of TBM Avengers for civilian forest fire fighting operations. Other World War II types that were stored there until the 1950's include the Boeing PB-1(B-17), Convair PBY-6A, Goodyear FG-1, Grumman F6F, Grumman F8F and Vought F4U.

In 1965 Litchfield Park was closed and the operation combined with the USAF at Davis-Monthan Air Force Base where both Navy and Air Force planes have been stored continually to this date.

NAS Norfolk

In 1946 the Naval Air Station at Norfolk, Virginia, became the center of salvage operations for naval aviation. The Public Works Department designed and built a large guillotine to speed up the slow work of cutting up planes by hand with acetylene torches. A large blade made from two thicknesses of two-inch armor plate, weighing 6,100 pounds, was mounted on a frame so that it could be dropped from a height of 26 feet. This was adequate to chop through a fuselage or a plane's wings or tail up to 17 feet wide. The previous system took one man a full day to cut up one aircraft, whereas the new system enabled a production rate of 16 planes a day.

The sections cut up were put into melting pots that reduced them to aluminum ingots, which were sold to buyers throughout the U.S. In fiscal 1947, a total of 297 railroad cars (nine million pounds) were shipped for sale, and in the first eight months of 1948 161 additional railroad cars were filled. The Salvage Yard ran three eight-hour shifts and over a three year period the record was the production of 21,675 pounds of ingots in one 24-hour period.

Douglas R4D-1, 4700, at Oakland, CA, on December 1, 1946. It is typical of the appearance of the surplus DC-3s at the end of the war. This one became NC-36898.

A Brewster SB2A-4 at Bush Field, Georgia, in February 1946. PV-2s, PB4Y-1s and F4Fs can be seen in the background. (Warren Bodie)

Waco YKS-6, NC-16210, to Navy 09783. Typical of the large number of small airplanes that were impressed into the service in Alaska early in World War II. This plane was assigned to NAS Sitka in June 1942 and sold surplus to become N236D. (Arthur Geen)

Boeing 314B, NC-18609, for sale at Floyd Bennett Field in New York in 1946. It was one of the Pan American Airlines Clippers that were given paper Navy Bureau Numbers and operated by PAA during the war. Universal Airlines bought this one and five others for $352,000. (Harold Martin)

A Martin PBM-5 with the ultimate in post-war graffiti. The plane's name is "Carol Ann 3." The lettering on the wing float is "Lucky Bag MAA Shack," and the fuselage is adorned with such comments as "Present to Mick, St. Louis, MO," "Officers Country, Restricted To Men," "Kilroy Took A Pro In This Plane," "Sayonara" and "Aloha Nui Mokohoi." The name "Ace Campbell" is under the pilot's window. Photographed in the "boneyard" at NAS Alameda on July 29, 1946.

Civil Aircraft Impressments

Private pre-war civilian aircraft were sold or given to the Navy in the same fashion as those taken over by the AAF. However, information on these is much more difficult to find and most of the following data is from the individual aircraft history cards that only show the aircraft as "stricken" with no indication as to whether or not it was sold.

Other sources verify the sale of former Pan American Airways planes. The Boeing 314 flying boats have been publicized, but there was a fairly large group of Pan Am planes in Alaska that were taken over by the Navy. How many of these were sold back to civilians as government surplus is not known. Some were operated by their civilian designation, such as Waco VKS-7, BuNo 37649, used by Pan American Airways at Sherman Field, California, for instrument flight checks. If a Navy model designation was assigned, it is in parenthesis.

American Pilgrim 100
Beech 17 (GB-1, GB-2)
Beech 18
Bellanca CH-300
Boeing 314
Consolidated 28 (PBY-4)
Fairchild 24 (GK-1, GQ-1)
Douglas DC-3
Douglas DC-5 (R3D-3)
Grumman G-21A (JRF-4)
Grumman G-44 (J4F-2)
Howard DGA-11
Howard DGA-15 (GH-1)
Lockheed 10
Lockheed 18 (R5O-3)
Martin M-130
Rearwin 8135
Sikorsky S-40 (RS-4)
Sikorsky S-42 (RS-5)
Stinson Junior SR
Stinson Reliant SR-9B
Stinson Reliant SR-10F
Vought-Sikorsky VS-44A (JR2S-1)
Waco VKS-7
Waco YKS-6
Waco YKS-7

Piper AE-1, 30288, at Concord in November 1946. Operating as a small ambulance plane, the rear fuselage top opened as shown to allow placement of a litter with a patient.

Grumman J2F-4, 1649, on its ferry flight from Dos Palos to Concord on December 22, 1946. It became NC-63850 and was undergoing complete restoration in 2004.

Cessna JRC-1, 64464, surplus from NAS Alameda. Although the AAF AT-17s and UC-78s were common, a few Navy versions were sold surplus. This lineup is at San Jose, CA, in September 1945.

Vought F4U-1, 18047, in the weeds at Long Beach, California in May 1946.

**Grumman F4F-4, 12114, with the unusual markings "J1-F-7."
This Wildcat was in the Marine Corps Museum in 1996.**

Grumman JRF-2, V174, at Concord on January 21, 1947. This is the original first JRF-2 delivered to the Coast Guard in 1939. It was sold surplus as NC-68902.

Stearman N2S-3, 38016, at Concord in October 1946. Five of these were the first planes to arrive at this WAA sales center. An unusual feature of this plane is the canopy railing that was used for cold weather flying on the lend-lease Stearmans in Canada. Over 415 Navy Stearmans were offered for sale by WAA.

NAS Clinton

The largest Navy storage facility, as well as the largest in the United States, was the Naval Air Station at Clinton, Oklahoma. The 8,839 aircraft stored there in April 1946 far exceeded any of the AAF and WAA fields. The largest groups were Fighters 3,762; Trainers 1,495; and Scout-Bombers 1,478. The full list of types as of April 9, 1946 comprises:

Brewster F3A (F4U)	111
Canadian Car & Foundry SBW (SB2C)	95
Cessna JRC (UC-78)	2
Consolidated PBY-5A	1
Consolidated PB4Y	161
Consolidated RY	9
Curtiss SB2C	362
Curtiss SOC	3
Douglas SBD	933
Fairchild Aircraft of Canada SBF (SB2C)	88
General Motors (Eastern Aircraft) FM (F4F)	1,444
General Motors (Eastern Aircraft) TBM (TBF)	1,039
Goodyear FG (F4U)	404
Grumman F4F	2
Grumman F6F	1,366
Lockheed-Vega PV	316
Naval Aircraft Factory OS2N (OS2U)	62
North American PBJ (B-25)	331
Stearman (Boeing) N2S	344
Vought-Sikorsky F4U	435
Vought-Sikorsky OS2U	180
Vultee SNV (BT-13)	1,151

Of all of the Vultee trainers used during World War II the SNV-2 (Navy BT-13B) is the least known. This photo shows 44071 at San Jose, CA, in March 1946.

Interstate TDR-1, 64507, NX-77980C at Tulare, CA, in July 1960. This piloted radio-controlled drone was an unusual surplus item. Employees of the air tanker operator TBM Inc. at the field told photographers as a joke that it was to be made into a fire-fighting air tanker.

General Motors TBM-1C, 46122, to NX-9394H. Operated by Paul Mantz as "Weath-Air Inc." for cloud seeding research. It later became the first TBM Air Tanker in the U.S. Photo at Phoenix, Arizona, on May 11, 1948.

Chapter 3

ONTARIO, CALIFORNIA

Cal-Aero Academy at Ontario, California, was one of the first civilian "AAF Contract Pilot Schools" along with the Rankin Aero Academy at Tulare, California. These were started in 1941 to meet the urgent demand for Air Corps pilot training that could not be provided by the service at the time. Cal-Aero was both a Primary (Stearmans) and Basic (BT-13s) Training Field that was closed in late 1944 when the demand for primary flight training was diminishing.

It is located 40 miles East of Los Angeles, six miles South of Ontario and 4-1/2 miles SE of Chino. Because there was also the Ontario Army Air Field (Ontario AAF) with operational P-38s etc., there has been some confusion about the RFC/WAA site. Ontario AAF is now Ontario International Airport and Cal-Aero Field is now Chino Airport.

The 1944 runway of 4,700 feet at Cal-Aero Field has been extended to 6,200 feet and Chino Airport is now the home of the largest warbird

An overall view of Cal-Aero Field, Ontario (now Chino Airport), California on May 22, 1946. Most of the WAA storage area is shown with P-39s, P-38s, B-26s and B-24s in the foreground.

activity in the United States with two aviation museums, restoration companies and individual aircraft owners. The Air Museum-Planes of Fame (Ed Maloney) holds frequent flying and ground displays and the Yanks Air Museum (Charles Nichols) displays many World War II planes, including the rare Curtiss O-52, as well as additional aircraft undergoing restoration.

The availability of a large inactive field in 1945 provided the RFC with an excellent storage facility. Because it was identified as "Ontario Primary Flying School" by the Army-Navy Directory of Airfields and navigation charts the name Ontario was used by all RFC/WAA sales literature even though it was closer to Chino than Ontario.

Surplus aircraft began to arrive, rising to a total of at least 1,906 by January 1946. After sales by War Assets this had been reduced to 1,390 by the time that Sharp & Fellows Contracting Company of Los Angeles was given the exclusive contract to dispose of them. The variety of types included the following:

Aeronca TG-5; Beech AT-10; Bell P-39; Boeing B-17; Cessna AT-17, C-78, JRC-1; Consolidated B-24, PB4Y; Consolidated PBY-5A; Curtiss A-25; Curtiss C-46; Curtiss P-40; Douglas A-20, P-70; Douglas A-24; Douglas C-47, R4D; Douglas C-54; Fairchild AT-21; Grumman J2F-4, J2F-6; Grumman TBF; Lockheed A-29, AT-18; Lockheed C-60, R5O-6; Lockheed P-38, P-400; Lockheed-Vega B-34, B-37; Martin B-26; North American A-36; North American AT-6; North American B-25; North American O-47; North Am,erican P-51; Northrop P-61; Piper J-5; Piper L-4; Republic P-43; Republic P-47; Stinson L-1; Taylorcraft TG-6; Vultee BT-13 and Waco CG-15.

The Smelters at Kingman, Walnut Ridge, Ontario, Clinton and Altus were designed by the Aircraft Conversion Company who also hired the metallurgists to operate them,. Kingman had three furnaces, Walnut Ridge and Clinton each had two, and Altus and Ontario each had one.

One of the differences at Ontario was that the smelter was not on the field as it was at the other locations. The planes were cut up on the airport and the parts then trucked to the furnace at Norco, nine miles southeast of Chino. This added an additional cost of $.0095 per pound to the ingots.

Recovery of Aluminum was the main purpose and Ontario produced 7,744,000 pounds from the smelter that sold for $676, 776. An additional recovery of five million pound s of aluminum tubing, brass, copper, lead, magnesium, plexiglass, steel and rubber, plus 3,375 gallons of gasoline and oil, was accomplished at Cal-Aero Field.

Stripped P-38s and B-24s without engines could be seen from Euclid Avenue on the West side of Cal-Aero Field in 1946.

A closeup of the group of A-20s and P-70s sitting on their tails with no engines.

Stripped Bell P-39s, on the left, and Douglas A-20s and P-70s on the right at Ontario.

A group of Curtiss C-46s can be seen above neat rows of removable parts.

A group of B-24s is in the left center of the photo.

A ground view of the A-20s and P-70s as seen from Merrill Avenue in the Northeast corner of the field in May 1946.

Blunt nosed P-70s without their engines as seen from Merrill Avenue outside of the field.

Actor Dana Andrews and Bell P-39s in an advertising photo for the RKO 1946 motion picture "The Best Years of Our Lives." (James Farmer Collection)

Douglas A-20G-45-DO, 43-22221, on the ramp in front of the hangars. A C-54 may be seen in the left background.

Curtiss A-25A-20-CS, 42-79765. These were AAF versions of the Navy SB2C-3.

Lockheed RA-29B, 41-23425, with the rudder from 41-23351. Delivered to Ontario from Tinker Field on April 3, 1945.

North American A-36A-1-NA, 42-83721. This was the dive bomber version of the P-51A fighter. Delivered from Buckley Field, Colorado, to RFC Ontario on March 19, 1945.

Lockheed AT-18, 42-55629, from Gila Bend AAF in Arizona. (John C. Mitchell)

Martin TB-26B-MA, 42-95663, with a P-47 in the left background.

Martin B-26B-35-MA, 41-32031, with very worn camouflage paint.

Ford-built B-24H-1-FO, 42-7580, with a modified nose and turrets removed.

North American B-25C-1-NA, 41-13266.

Ford-built RB-24E-26-FO, 42-7341. The higher angle was obtained by standing on the roof of my Model B Ford.

Curtiss C-46A-35-CU, 42-3649, with the Air Transport Command insignia.

Curtiss C-46A-35-CU, 42-3644, with the ATC insignia and its wheels half sunk into the ground.

Curtiss C-46E-1-CS, 43-47419, returned from the Chinese Air Force. It became NC-30019 and then went to Mexico as XB-LIU. (Gordon S. Williams)

Lockheed P-38F, 41-7524.

Lockheed P-38F, 41-2302. The P-38 is a difficult plane to photograph and this photo from the roof of my Model B Ford is a different angle.

Lockheed P-38G-10-LO, 41-3488.

Lockheed P-38G-15-LO, 43-2359, with drop tanks under the center section. A Douglas A-24 is in the left background.

Lockheed P-38H-5-LO, 42-66948, in a row of P-38s at Ontario. Delivered to Ontario RFC from Santa Maria April 17, 1945. This plane had been assigned to Ontario AAF in June 1944.

Bell P-39Q-15-BE, 44-2352, one of the few P-39's that had not been stripped. The belly tank and wheels are hidden by the high grass of this area.

Curtiss P-40F, 41-14156.

Curtiss P-40M-1-CU, 43-5403. Delivered from Luke Field on March 24, 1945.

Curtiss P-40K-1-CU, 42-46216, with a rudder from another P-40. The Luke Field side number X845A, just like the plane, is fading away. Delivered to Ontario March 10, 1945.

Douglas P-70A-1-DO, 42-53543, an A-20G modified as a night fighter. Martin B-26s are in the background. Delivered from Hammer Field to Ontario RFC on March 31, 1945.

Douglas P-70B-2-DO, 43-10230, painted black all over. Based at Hammer Field and Salinas AAF, delivered to Ontario on February 22, 1945.

Douglas P-70B, 42-54053, an A-20G modified. Delivered from Salinas, CA, to Ontario RFC on February 26, 1945.

Douglas TP-70B-2-DO, 43-10003. Delivered from Hammer Field, Fresno, CA, on March 27, 1945.

Republic P-47D-11-RA, 42-23007, in natural metal finish. Delivered from Sweetwater, Texas, to Ontario on August 10, 1945.

Navy Grumman J2F-4, 1643, at Ontario on May 22, 1946.

North American P-51C-1-NT, 43-25057, with an insignia painted out on the rear fuselage.

A Navy Consolidated PBY-5A, 04994, at Ontario.

Douglas R4D-5-30-DK, 17247. The Model Designation was an interesting combination of Navy R4D-5 and AAF C-47A-30-DK.

A Marine Corps Lockheed R5O-5, 39617, with Vultee BT-13s in the background.

Grumman TBF-1, 06125, coded "S45" with the YP-61 in the left rear. (John C. Mitchell)

Northrop YP-61, 41-18887, one of two WP-61s at Ontario. B-26s without engines sit on their tails in the right background in November 1945. (John C. Mitchell)

Chapter 4

KINGMAN, ARIZONA

The size and scope of the 5,540 aircraft at Kingman, Arizona, in 1946 could only be seen and understood from the air. Even this photo, taken on February 8, 1947 does not show all of the aircraft there at that time.

By far the best known of the World War II surplus fields because of wide publicity over the years was the former Kingman AAF in Arizona. Built during the war as a gunnery training field, it provided a large area for storage in dry air and good weather. This was the initial purpose of Kingman — to temporarily store flyable bombers and other aircraft from Europe for expected use in the Pacific Theater for the invasion of Japan.

At its peak operation, Kingman AAF was a Main Base of the Western Flying Training Command with a Special 4-engine Co-Pilot (B-17) School and a Flexible Gunnery School. It had housing for 430 Officers, 3070 Cadets and 3200 Enlisted Men. It had three runways, the longest of which was 6,800 feet. It had seven auxiliary fields under its command plus two gunnery and bombing ranges. Training ended in April 1945 and the base was placed on standby status.

With the sudden end of the war the mission of Kingman AAF was changed to that of a storage base and eventually a salvage field to be operated by a private contractor. In September 1945 the AAF San Bernardino Air Technical Service Command entered into an agreement with the RFC that resulted in setting up Sales Depot No. 41 and an organization to operate the field for this purpose. By October there were 50 Officers and 1,300 Enlisted Men assigned. The Parking Crew spotted and parked the aircraft as they landed. The Strippers took over and removed all equipment that was termed combat, restricted or Confidential. That included bombsights, guns, ammunition, radar equipment, pyrotechnics (flares, Very pistols, etc.). Then the Taxi Crew taxied the plane to a designated area for storage. The Storage Crew led the plane from the concrete ramp and taxiways to the storage area. The equipment was removed from the plane and turned over to the Inspection

Surplus WWII U.S. Aircraft

A closer view of the main part of the storage area from a lower altitude. The 1929 city airport built for the transcontinental TAT air-rail route is at the top center of the photo and is where the author rented a Piper Cub J-3C to take these photos.

Kingman, Arizona

Department where it was tagged, packed, crated and shipped to an AAF Air Depot warehouse.

The first planes started to arrive on October 10, 1945. At one period in November, between 100 and 150 planes a day would be delivered, but this decreased to about 43 planes per day by late December. The total number delivered as of December 31, 1945 was 4,693. Most of the AAF personnel had left for Victorville AAF by November, so the Reconstruction and Finance employees started to do some of the work. By the end of December the military staff was down to 15 Officers and 266 Enlisted Men. Gradually the AAF stopped taxiing the planes and by the end of December the RFC took over completely.

One of the most frustrating things for recent historians and enthusiasts who have never been able to find records of the planes at Kingman is this official statement:

"Included under Maintenance was the Record Section that reported every storage aircraft to Washington and Wright Field. This report included the type and number of the plane, condition of airplane and engines, type and serial number of engines, and type and serial number of each propeller hub and propeller blade. This section also made shipping tickets on each airplane so that the RFC representative on the base could sign for the planes as they arrived."

Active duty aircraft were flown in by military crews and parked for civilian employees to move to storage locations throughout the many acres of open area. Toward the end of this operation new planes from factories such as Consolidated were delivered from the production flight line to Kingman to be scrapped.

North American B-25D-35-NC, RAF FW267. These were used by the RCAF, and this one was returned from Montreal in November 1945. It was built as AAF Serial Number 43-3703 and assigned to Lend-Lease in Canada.

BOMB GROUPS REPRESENTED AT KINGMAN

An incomplete but extensive list of aircraft at Kingman derived from a study of all available aerial and ground photos taken in 1946 and 1947:

Bomb Group	Aircraft	Air Force	Identification
2nd	B-17	15th	Y in circle
11th	B-24	7th	Solid triangle (26 BS)
11th	B-24	7th	Solid square (41 BS)
43rd	B-24	5th	Diagonal bar and rudder stripes
44th	B-24	8th	Vertical stripe & underline
90th	B-24	5th	Skull and crossed bombs
91st	B-17	8th	Triangle A
94th	B-17	8th	Square A
95th	B-17	8th	Square B
96th	B-17	8th	Square C
97th	B-17	15th	Y in triangle
99th	B-17	15th	Y in diamond
100th	B-17	8th	Square D
303rd	B-17	8th	Triangle C
305th	B-17	8th	Triangle G
307th	B-24	13th	LR
351st	B-17	8th	Triangle J
381st	B-17	8th	Triangle L
385th	B-17	8th	M and checkerboard
388th	B-17	8th	Square H
389th	B-24	8th	Vertical stripe
390th	B-17	8th	Square J
392nd	B-24	8th	Horizontal stripe
398th	B-17	8th	Triangle W
401st	B-17	8th	Triangle S
446th	B-24	8th	Horizontal stripe
447th	B-17	8th	Square K
448th	B-24	8th	Diagonal band
452nd	B-17	8th	Square L
457th	B-17	8th	Triangle U
459th	B-24	15th	Diamond and checkerboard
464th	B-24	15th	Square and vertical bar
465th	B-24	15th	Square and two bars
484th	B-24	15th	Horizontal X and colors
485th	B-24	15th	X and rectangle
486th	B-17	8th	Square W
487th	B-17	8th	Square P
492nd	B-24	8th	Diagonal band
494th	B-24	7th	Colored quarters
834th	B-17	8th	Triangle P
868th	B-24	13th	S in diamond

A portion of a larger view showing the YB-24Ns, the main hangar, barracks on the right and the smelters in left center. The tent city in the top right was built to house civilian workers employed by Wunderlich.

This ground view of B-24s shows how difficult it was to see more than a few planes at one time, so this required driving up and down the parked rows looking for interesting aircraft. The view on the ground in the middle of the 5,000 planes was very limited.

A sea of B-24s as far as the eye can see.

An aerial view from about 500 feet was a perfect altitude to see the massive array of B-24s

Next page: **The final altitude of about 200 feet was a thrilling ride alongside this awesome display of World War II combat veterans gleaming in the clear air and early morning Arizona sunshine.**

Surplus WWII U.S. Aircraft

Kingman, Arizona

Planes such as this black B-24 were hard to see on the ground but easy to spot from the air.

The last row of B-17s with interesting markings but no engines. The famous "Bit 'O Lace", 44-297976, is K-D next to the black B-17 in the front row. The main area with the B-24s can be seen on the far horizon.

Probably the most unusual type scrapped at Kingman was the Consolidated B-32. This view shows all of them grouped together. Some were new from the factory, some were TB-32s used to train flight crews.

The planes were generally sorted by type, as shown by this group of North American B-25s.

Surplus WWII U.S. Aircraft

Another view showing the B-32s in relation to the main body of planes in the upper left.

Douglas RA-24B-1-DT, 42-54288, at the edge of the field near the railroad tracks. This shows how close some of the planes were to the passenger trains passing by and why so many remember "seeing all those planes."

Douglas TA-20G-45-DO, 43-21657, with the insignia of the 650th Bomb Squadron at Florence AAF, South Carolina.

Douglas-built B-17G-70-DL, 44-6906, named "Constipated Lady". From the 390th Bomb Group, 570th Bomb Squadron. The higher angle of this photo was made possible by standing on an AAF Jeep.

Douglas TA-20G-45-DO, 43-21756, on its nose.
This plane was unusual for its unpainted condition.

Douglas TA-20H-1-DO, 44-23. By the end of the war most A-20s had been re-designated as Training planes. B-24s without engines can be seen on the left.

Douglas A-20H-10-DO, 44-308, with its belly tank.

Douglas TA-20J-15-DO, 43-21558.

Douglas TA-20J-15-DO, 43-21704. The A-20s may have had weak nose gears that collapsed after being towed over rough ground to their storage area.

Douglas TA-20K-15-DO, 44-731. It was assigned to the 46th Bomb Group, 87th Bomb Squadron, at Morris Field and shows their Winged Horse insignia on the nose.

Douglas-built B-17F-30-DL, 42-3182. This is the only "F" model that I saw at Kingman, and it was in very good condition.

Vega-built B-17G-15-VE, 42-97510, with the markings of the 384th Bomb Group, 546th Bomb Squadron.

Vega-built B-17G-5-VE, 42-39926, named "Holey Joe". The name under the top turret was "Shirley".

Boeing B-17G-40-BO, 42-97123, from the 457th Bomb Group.

Douglas-built B-17G-50-DL, 44-6315, named "Fearless F" from the 487th Bomb Group.

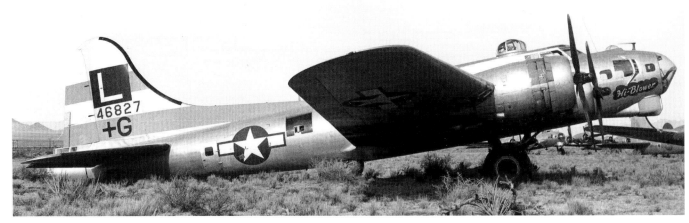

Douglas-built B-17G-65-DL, 44-6827, named "Hi-Blower." Coded "KG-G" from the 452nd Bomb Group, 730th Bomb Squadron — all the way from England to Arizona.

Vega-built B-17G-80-VE, 44-8745, from the 94th Bomb Group.

Douglas-built B-17G-95-DO, 43-38738, named "Be Comin Back." It flew 57 Missions with the 401st Bomb Group, 614th Bomb Squadron.

Boeing B-17G-70-BO, 43-37716. This famous plane was named "Five Grand" for being the 5,000th B-17 built by Boeing, and carried the signatures of Boeing workers all over the plane, from nose to tail. It flew 78 missions with the 96th Bomb Group, 338th Bomb Squadron.

Consolidated TB-24J-66-CO, 42-100052, named "Gangrene Gertie."
The nose has been modified by the removal of the turret.

446th BG

Consolidated B-24J-205-CO, 44-41315, named "Uncle Jim."

Consolidated RLB-30, AL594, modified from the early LB-30 bomber configuration for the Royal Air Force to a C-87 type passenger plane for the Air Transport Command. The ATC insignia is to the left of the star and bar. Delivered to Kingman January 7, 1946.

459th BG

Consolidated RB-24A, 40-2364, modified as a transport. This was so rare that I had to photograph it even if it did not have any propellers.

Consolidated B-24J-208-CO, 44-41331, named "Princess Carol".

446th BG

Ford-built RB-24L-11-FO, 44-49630, modified with the B-29 Central Fire Control system for training B-29 crews. It was from Las Vegas AAF and delivered to Kingman on December 19, 1945.

Consolidated B-24M-40-CO, 44-42606, with a modified nose and radar bar under the fuselage.

389th BG

Consolidated C-87-2-CO, 42-6985.

Surplus WWII U.S. Aircraft

Consolidated B-24J-190-CO, 44-40973, named "The Dragon and his Tail" from the 43rd Bomb Group, 5th Air Force. This remarkable art work was all the way down the fuselage. It was one of the last planes to be scrapped at Kingman and requests to save it failed. In recent years the Collings Foundation B-24J was painted with a very accurate rendition of this, so that thousands have now been able to see what it was like. (Peter M. Bowers)

North American B-25D-35-NC, 43-3666, named "The Purple Shaft." This was an interesting modification with an H tail turret and under fuselage radome.

North American B-25D Mitchell II, RAF FW247, returned to the U.S. in November 1945.

North American TB-25H-10-NO, 43-4897, Trainer without its 75mm nose cannon.

Martin TB-26B-35-MA, 41-32033.

Martin TB-26B-35-MA, 41-32012, with the "BA" Training Field markings of Barksdale. Delivered to Kingman on November 22, 1945.

Martin TB-26B-10-MA, 41-18214.

Martin TB-26C-21-MO, 41-35153. Note the stacked propellers in the background to the right.

Martin TB-26B-40-MO, 42-43332. The neat rows of props on the left and engines on right show the organized salvage of parts that were removed before the fuselage, wings and tail were cut up and pushed into the furnaces.

Martin RB-26B-40-MO, 42-43347.

Martin RB-26B-40-MO, 42-43338. The "R" model designation prefix was used late in the war to denote Restricted use of a combat plane.

B-26G-10-MA, 43-34543, from Barksdale Field in Louisiana.

Martin TB-26C-45-MO, 42-107495. Fiscal Year 1942 had the highest aircraft production for the AAF so that some serial numbers were exceedingly long. The last digit of the Fiscal Year was used with the individual serial number so that "2107495" was painted on this B-26.

Martin TB-26C-20-MO, 41-35098. The "T" model designation prefix indicated a former combat type plane modified for Training use. This usually meant the removal of all armament and turrets. Two F-5 photo versions of the P-38 can be seen on the left.

Consolidated B-32-1-CF, 42-108480.

Convair TB-32-10-CF, 42-108500. Delivered to Kingman on December 13, 1945 and damaged while being towed over rough ground to the middle of the field.

Consolidated B-32-20-CF, 42-108537. The "CF" indicated that the plane was built at the Convair plant at Fort Worth, Texas.

Lockheed F-5E-4-LO, 44-24560, photo-reconnaissance version of the P-38. The large oblique camera window is visible in the nose.

North American RF-6C-10-NT, 44-10911. The camera port is just below the rear bar of the national insignia. The railroad tracks on the edge of the field are on the left.

Republic P-47D-4-RA, 42-22729.

Curtiss TP-40N-30-CU, 44-7068, two-place Trainer version of the P-40N. From Punta Gorda AAF to Kingman on December 15, 1945.

Curtiss TP-40N-35-CU, 44-7541.

Curtiss P-40R, 41-13659, from Luke Field to Kingman, November 7, 1945.

Curtiss TP-40R, 41-13682, from Luke Field to Kingman on October 25, 1945.

Bell P-63A-6-BE, 42-69013, with an unusual paint scheme of a green fuselage and lightning bolt.

Bell RP-63A-9-BE, 42-69501. Delivered from Pyote AAF to Kingman on November 1, 1945. P-63s can be seen on the left and right. In January 1946 there were 119 at Kingman.

Bell P-63A-9-BE, 42-69425. The insignia on the nose reads "Aeroprop Test #3, Aeroproducts Flight Test."

Bell RP-63A-6-BE, 42-68959.

Surplus WWII U.S. Aircraft

Twin-Engine Cessna Airplanes
$3900 TO $8500

Sale of Government Surplus Property Through Reconstruction Finance Corporation

A large, comfortable cabin, coupled with twin-engine safety, and the ability to get in and out of small airports give this airplane general utility value.

It operates on 73 octane gasoline and cruises at approximately 140 m.p.h. This plane is suitable for business transportation, light cargo, pilot training, or personal use.

This aircraft is a low-wing monoplane of composite wood, steel and fabric construction and is powered with two Jacobs Model L4MB engines, of 225 horsepower each. These Army models, designated as UC-78 and AT-17 (commercial model T-50), are type-certificated but individual planes must be repaired and modified to meet Civil Aeronautics Administration airworthiness requirements for civilian flight.

Information concerning sales procedure, location of aircraft, and price, may be obtained from your nearest Sales Center.

PRICE DETERMINATION
Prices for these planes have been set to make allowances toward modifications, repairs and overhaul. The $8500 price is for planes equipped with constant speed propellers, and a wing which is eligible for CAA approval to permit a 5400 pound gross weight. Prices are lower for planes equipped with fixed pitch wood propellers and/or a wing designed for a 5100 pound gross weight.

SALES CENTERS
(Cities listed alphabetically by States)

LOCATION	AIRPORT
Birmingham, Alabama	Municipal
Phoenix, Arizona	Thunderbird II
Tucson, Arizona	Ryan
Wickenburg, Arizona	Echeverria
Pine Bluff, Arkansas	Grider
West Helena, Arkansas	Thompson-Robbins
Blythe, California	Gary
Concord, California	Sherman
Fresno, California	Chandler Field
Hemet, California	Ryan
Ontario, California	Cal-Aero
Denver, Colorado	Rutledge
Miami, Florida	Chapman
St. Petersburg, Florida	Ludwig-Sky Harbor
Americus, Georgia	Souther
Augusta, Georgia	Bush
Douglas, Georgia	Municipal
Lansing, Illinois	Ford-Lansing
Indianapolis, Indiana	Sky Harbor
Davenport, Iowa	Cran
Wichita, Kansas	Municipal
Baton Rouge, Louisiana	E. Baton Rouge Parish
North Grafton, Massachusetts	North Grafton
Lansing, Michigan	Capitol City
Minneapolis, Minnesota	Victory
Clarksdale, Mississippi	Fletcher
Madison, Mississippi	Augustine
Cape Girardeau, Missouri	Harris
Kansas City, Missouri	Municipal
Robertson, Missouri	Municipal
Sikeston, Missouri	Harvey Park
Helena, Montana	Municipal
Omaha, Nebraska	Municipal
Reno, Nevada	Reno
Readington, New Jersey	Solberg-Hunterton
Albuquerque, New Mexico	Army Air Field
Albany, New York	Albany
Rochester, New York	Municipal
White Plains, New York	Westchester County
Charlotte, North Carolina	Cannon
Akron, Ohio	Municipal
Cincinnati, Ohio	Lunkin
Muskogee, Oklahoma	Hat Box
Oklahoma City, Oklahoma	Cimarron
Ponca City, Oklahoma	Municipal
Portland, Oregon	Portland-Troutdale
Pittsburgh, Pennsylvania	Bettis
Bennettsville, South Carolina	Palmer
Camden, South Carolina	Woodward
Sioux Falls, South Dakota	Sioux
Jackson, Tennessee	McKellar
Union City, Tennessee	Embry-Riddle
Ballinger, Texas	Bruce
Corsicana, Texas	Corsicana
Cuero, Texas	Municipal
Fort Stockton, Texas	Gibbs
Fort Worth, Texas	Hicks
Houston, Texas	Municipal
Lamesa, Texas	Lamesa
San Antonio, Texas	Municipal
Stamford, Texas	Arledge
Vernon, Texas	Victory
Salt Lake City, Utah	Municipal No. 1
Alexandria, Virginia	Hybla Valley
Morgantown, West Virginia	Municipal

RECONSTRUCTION FINANCE CORPORATION
A DISPOSAL AGENCY DESIGNATED BY THE SURPLUS PROPERTY BOARD

16-2

Chapter 5

DELAYED SALES

The full story of the retention and sale of World War II aircraft types does not end with the closing down of the War Assets Administration and its sales facilities shortly after the war, because the AAF and the Navy placed some of these planes in preserved storage or released them for sale after normal service in the 1950's and 1960's.

There is no master list of these types, but the photographs in this Chapter will give a good indication of what was available. The sale of a large number of North American P-51Ds in November 1957 is the best known example of this, but of equal importance was the release of a large number of General Motors TBM Avengers which then formed the basis of the new civilian fleet of forest fire fighting air tankers. Further modifications to air tankers took place as a result of the release of PBYs, PV-2s and some surplus Coast Guard P4Y-2Gs.

Boeing P2B-2S, Navy 84031, at Van Nuys, California, in August 1949.

Beech C-45F, N8048H, at Concord, CA, in December 1956. It was one of seven purchased in 1956.

Consolidated PBY-6A, N64T, purchased by Glenn "Red" Turner in 1956. The faded "T" on the tail shows its former assignment to the Naval Reserve at Seattle, Washington.

North American AT-6D, N9517C, 42-85048, at San Francisco in October 1956. This late sale of a World War II plane shows the required painting out of the military markings and a quick hand-painted registration on the nose.

Lockheed-Vega PV-1, Navy 34807, with the Royal Canadian Air Force serial number 2247. This is an example of a Lend-Lease plane sent to Canada and returned to the United States to be sold surplus. At Long Beach, CA, in March 1953.

Douglas B-19A at Wright Field in 1947. It has the All Weather Flying Service markings and David Bowers in the foreground. It was sold to Mobile Smelters in Tucson, Arizona, in 1949 and reduced to aluminum ingots. (Peter M. Bowers)

Northrop F-15A, N9768Z, 45-59300. Sold surplus by the NACA Laboratory at Moffett Field, it was modified into a forest fire fighting air tanker. It is shown here as operated by Aero Enterprises at Fresno, CA, in November 1965.

Surplus WWII U.S. Aircraft

General Motors TBM-3U, N104Z, at Concord, CA, in December 1956. Eight of these TBM-3Us were overhauled and painted by the Navy at NAS Norfolk for transfer to the U. S. Forest Service where they were evaluated for use as air tankers.

North American P-51D, N5441V, 45-11582, from the sale at McClellan Field in November 1957. This photo was taken at Sacramento Airport on November 6th just before B. C. Reed flew it to Ontario for Ed Maloney. Michael Coutches bought 24 and had six barged down the Sacramento River to Oakland Airport. (Boardman C. Reed)

Douglas B-26C, N2852G, 44-35493, at Concord, CA, in May 1958. Another B-26, N7662C, is to the left.

Douglas R5D-4R, N96358, Navy 90398, as Tanker 160 running up on the end of the runway at Porterville, CA, in 1999. (Milo Peltzer)

Fairchild C-82A, N4833V, 44-23031, at Hayward, CA, in September 1955. (Lawrence S. Smalley)

Consolidated P4Y-2G, N6813D, Navy-Coast Guard 59876, weather-beaten sprayer at Boise, Idaho, in August 1966. The P4Y-2G designation was used by the U. S. Coast Guard for their modified PB4Y-2s. (Boardman C. Reed)

Boeing YC-97, 45-59590, at Fairfield-Suisun AAF in August 1947. This was sold surplus and became N9538C, going to Israel in 1964.

Douglas C-74, N3183G, 42-65412. At Long Beach, CA, in July 1960, with the remains of its MATS markings on the tail.

Martin PBM-5A, N3190G, Navy 122071, in semi-derelict condition at Porterville, CA, in February 1959. After years of volunteer work it is now on display in good condition at the Pima Air Museum in Arizona. (William L. Swisher)

Beech Expeditor, RCAF 1408, at Salinas, CA, in December 1968. This late surplus sale of rebuilt wartime C-45s in Canada is probably the final date for World War II surplus sales. This was one of 35 to 40 ex RCAF Beech 18s and Douglas C-47s bought by Pacific Air Lanes, a proposed mail carrier.

Grumman F8F-2, N7826C, Navy 121699, from the Naval Reserve at Jacksonville, Florida. Another F8F-2, N7827C (121752) is behind it. Both were at Buchanan Field, Concord, CA, on October 4, 1958. This is probably the last and newest World War II type to be sold surplus.

WAA-AE-921

BILL OF SALE
for
AIRCRAFT   Sales Document No. 5016425

341529

KNOW ALL MEN BY THESE PRESENTS:

That the UNITED STATES OF AMERICA, by and through the WAR ASSETS ADMINISTRATOR, under and pursuant to Executive Order 9689, dated January 31, 1946, and the powers and authority contained in the provisions of the Surplus Property Act of 1944 (58 Stat. 765) and SPR Regulation No. 1, as amended (11 F.R. 409), who has a Regional Office located at 39 Van Ness Avenue, San Francisco, California, has for disposal the following described property owned by the United States of America and which has been declared to be surplus property pursuant to said Surplus Property Act of 1944:

Army or Navy Identification Number	Aircraft Manufacturer and Model	Mfr's Serial Number	Mfr's Model Number
07923	Boeing N2S-3	75-7527	B75-N-1

NOW, THEREFORE, for and in consideration of the sum of Four Hundred and No/100 - Dollars ($ 400.00), cash in hand paid, receipt of which is hereby acknowledged, the UNITED STATES OF AMERICA, acting by and through the WAR ASSETS ADMINISTRATOR, does hereby sell, assign, transfer, and deliver, without covenant, warranty or representation, express or implied, of any nature whatsoever, all of its right, title and interest in and to the above-described surplus property, together with all appurtenances attached to or installed therein, unto Doris Eveline Lehman

whose address is Box 379, Route 1, Martinez, California

its (or his) successors and assigns, to have and to hold all and singular the said surplus property forever.

IN WITNESS WHEREOF, the UNITED STATES OF AMERICA, acting by and through the WAR ASSETS ADMINISTRATOR, has executed this instrument this 17th day of February, 1947

UNITED STATES OF AMERICA
By War Assets Administrator

By S. Raymond Burns, Director
Aircraft & Electronics Division

STATE OF CALIFORNIA
CITY AND COUNTY OF SAN FRANCISCO } SS:

On this 17th day of February, in the year 1947, before me, a notary public in and for the City and County of San Francisco, State of California, residing therein, duly commissioned and sworn, personally appeared S. Raymond Burns known to me to be the Director, Aircraft & Electronics Division of the War Assets Administrator and also known to me to be the person whose name is subscribed to the within instrument as the Director, Aircraft & Electronics Division of the War Assets Administrator and acknowledged that he executed the same as Director, Aircraft & Electronics Division of the War Assets Administrator.

IN WITNESS WHEREOF, I have hereunto set my hand and affixed my official seal, at my office in said City and County of San Francisco, the day and year in this certificate first above written.

(NOTARIAL SEAL)

Notary Public in and for the City and County of San Francisco, State of California

My Commission Expires August 27, 1947

Chapter 6

APPROVED TYPE CERTIFICATES

The Air Commerce Act of 1926 created for the first time in the United States a regulatory and licensing system for pilots and aircraft. Prior to that time there were no government standards or regulations even though both pilots and planes were actively operating.

A complete system for inspection and approval of aircraft was established by the new Bureau of Air Commerce division of the Department of Commerce. The standard certification "C" was added to the national identification letter "N" for United States. This registration combination of "NC" was in effect from 1927 to 1948.

The first Approved Type Certificate (ATC-1) was issued in March 1927 for the Buhl-Verville CA-3, and the system has continued from the Bureau of Air Commerce through the Civil Aeronautics Administration to the present Federal Aviation Administration. ATC's are issued only for production aircraft for which detailed inspections and approvals have been undertaken.

In order to qualify, the factory had to provide design details and drawings, and one sample plane submitted for a flight test. If the design and construction of the aircraft and its performance characteristics were found to be satisfactory then a Type Certificate was issued for that particular manufacturer and model.

To insure that aircraft of this model were made in conformity with the type certificate, the government agency carefully examined the factory, manufacturing equipment and inspection system of the manufacturer. If this was all satisfactory, a production certificate was issued. Production of that model then began in accordance with the approved specifications and a certified statement by the manufacturer that each individual aircraft was made in accordance with the specifications in the type certificate. A final visual inspection of each aircraft by a government representative determined that an airworthiness certificate could be issued for each individual aircraft.

The CAA has been very careful to identify wartime production of the same design by more than one manufacturer so that the ATC is specific to that company. This is best shown in the certification of the Warner powered Fairchild M-62B. The Fairchild production is listed as PT-23, those built by Aeronca as PT-23-AE, those built by Howard as PT-23-HO and those built by St. Louis as PT-23-SL. Those built by Fleet Aircraft of Canada (PT-23-FE) were not eligible for licensing.

Thus, any surplus military aircraft that was of the same type as a previously approved civilian model could be licensed under that category and operate with an NC registration. The extensive list of types is arranged by ATC Number.

243	Cessna UC-77
244	Cessna UC-77A
329	Stinson L-12A
384	Lockheed UC-101
530	Stinson L-12
551	Lockheed UC-36A, XR2O-1
558	Boeing C-73
573	Cessna UC-77B
579	Beech UC-43H
584	Lockheed R3O-1
591	Rearwin UC-102
598	Waco UC-72H
602	Beech UC-43G, UC-43J
603	Fairchild UC-88
604	Beech UC-43E
608	Stinson UC-81, UC-81L
609	Stinson UC-81B
610	Fairchild UC-61J
612	Howard UC-70C
616	Lockheed UC-40, UC-40A, JO-1, JO-2
618	Douglas C-49E, C-50, C-50A, C-50B, C-50C, C-50D, C-51, C-49, C-49A, C-49B, C-49C, C-49D, C-49J, C-49K, R4D-2
621	Stinson UC-81C, UC-81N
622	Cessna UC-77C, UC-77D
625	Stinson UC-81G, UC-81J, UC-81M
626	Waco UC-72K, UC-72M
627	Waco UC-72E
628	Spartan UC-71
633	Fairchild UC-61H
638	Beech UC-43A)
640	Stinson UC-81E
645	Howard UC-70A
648	Waco UC-72D
649	Beech UC-43, UC-43B, GB-1, GB-2
654	Grumman OA-9, JRF-1, JRF-2, JRF-3, JRF-4, JRF-5, JRF-6B
659	Harlow UC-80
663	Fairchild UC-61B
667	Fairchild UC-61E
669	Douglas C-47, C-47A, C-47B, C-48, C-48A, C-52, C-52A, C-52B, C-52C, C-53, C-53B, C-53C, C-53D, C-68, C-117A, R4D-1, R4D-3, R4D-4, R4D-5, R4D-6
671	Beech UC-43D
675	Aeronca L-3F
678	Stinson UC-81K
679	Stinson UC-81H
685	Stinson UC-81F
689	Beech UC-43C
691	Piper L-4, L-4A, L-4B, L-4H, L-4K, NE-1, NE-2
692	Piper L-4D
698	Piper L-4C
699	Taylorcraft L-2G, L-2K
700	Taylorcraft L-2F, J-2J
701	Cessna UC-94
702	Aeronca L-3G
706	Fairchild UC-61C, UC-61K, UC-86
707	Fairchild UC-61, UC-61A, UC-61F, UC-61G
710	Beech C-45C
711	Rearwin UC-102A
713	Beech UC-43F
713	Beech UC-43F
714	Waco UC-72, UC-72A, UC-72C
715	Funk UC-92
717	Howard UC-70, UC-70B, GH-1, GH-2, GH-3, NH-1
722	Cessna AT-17, UC-78
723	Lockheed C-57, C-57B, C-59, C-60, C-60A, R5O-1, R5O-2, R5O-3, R5O-5, R5O-6
724	Fairchild PT-19, PT-19A, PT-19A-AE, PT-19A-SL, PT-19B, PT-19B-AE, PT-23, PT-23-AE, PT-23-HO, PT-23-SL, PT-23A, PT-23A-SL, PT-26, PT-26A, PT-26B
725	Piper L-4F, L-4G, AE-1, HE-1
728	Aeronca L-3, L-3D, L-3E, L-3J
734	Grumman OA-14, J4F-2
738	Stinson L-9B
740	Piper L-4E
743	Boeing-Stearman PT-13, PT-13A, PT-13B, PT-13C, PT-13D, PT-17, PT-17A, PT-18, PT-27, N2S-1, N2S-2, N2S-3, N2S-5
746	Taylorcraft L-2, L-2A, L-2B, L-2C, L-2D, L-2E, L-2M

748	Culver PQ-8
749	Ryan PT-22, PT-22A
751	Aeronca L-3B
754	Interstate L-6, YL-6
756	Budd C-93, RB-1
757	Beech C-45, C-45A, C-45B, C-45F, AT-7, AT-8A, AT-7B, AT-7C, JRB-1, JRB-2, JRB-3, JRB-4, SNB-2, SNB-2C
762	Douglas C-54, C-54A, C-54B, C-54C, C-54D, C-54E, C-65G, R5D-1, R5D-2, R5D-3, R5D-4
764	Stinson L-5, L-5B, L-5C, L-5D, L-5E, L-5G
772	Curtiss C-46A, C-46D, C-46E, C-46F (Slick Airways)
774	Stinson AT-19
786	Curtiss C-46E (Curtiss-Wright)
789	Curtiss C-46A, C-46D, C-46F (L. B. Smith)
808	Curtiss C-46F (Skyways International)

Grumman JRF-6B, Royal Navy FP514 (U.S. Navy 66336), for sale by WAA at Concord, CA, on January 9, 1947. It was sold as NC-95431 to Bay Valley Air Service who started a commuter airline with three surplus JRF-6Bs between San Francisco and Sacramento, CA. The large lettering on the nose is "W2AN."

Douglas C-47, NC-17085, 41-18678, operated by Standard Air Cargo. Pilot Joseph Goeller is flying it with one engine feathered at my request for a special photo. Photographed over San Francisco Bay on January 10, 1948.

A rare Stinson UC-81F, 42-38301, for sale by WAA at Sherman Field, Concord, CA, in April 1945. This SR-10F "Reliant" was owned before the war by the Gulf Oil Corporation at Pittsburgh, PA, as NC-18479. (Earl Holmquist)

Piper NE-1, Navy 26322, for sale by WAA at Concord, CA, in February 1947.

Cessna AT-17B, NC-67094, flying near Concord, CA, on March 16, 1947. The AT-17Bs and near duplicate UC-78s were inexpensive because of their wood and fabric construction.

Fairchild C-61A. A 1942 photo of a factory-fresh AAF production version of the Fairchild 24W. (Fairchild Aircraft & Engineering)

Howard-built Fairchild PT-23-HO, 42-49278, for sale by WAA at Westchester County Airport, New York, in August 1945. Surplus PT-17s and PT-19s are in the background.

Lockheed R5O-1, NC-54549, ex-Coast Guard V-188, of Transocean Air Lines at Oakland, CA, in July 1952. It was a standard Model 18-40 passenger plane easily certified under that Approved Type Certificate.

Grumman OA-14 "Widgeon", 44-52997, named "The Stud Duck". This was the eighth "Widgeon" built, in 1941, and was NC-28669. After wartime service in the AAF it was sold surplus as N1250N. Photographed at Oakland, CA, in January 1948.

Culver PQ-8, NC-41779. Date and location unknown. (Larkins Collection)

Stearman PT-27, NR-57374, 41-15576 and RCAF FD974. An agricultural sprayer owned and flown by Charles Metcalf who installed one of the first 450 hp Wasp engines in this Stearman. Photo at Sacramento, CA, on February 21, 1948.

Taylorcraft L-2M, NC-57724, 43-25867, being flown over Suisun Bay, CA, by Kenny Trahan who later retired as a United Air Lines Captain.

Ryan PT-22, NC-57024, at Sherman Field, Concord, CA on September 20, 1945.

Aeronca L-3B, 42-38483, for sale by WAA at Sherman Field in January 1944. (John Larkins)

Budd RB-1, NC-45354, ex-Navy "Connestoga" at Oakland, CA, on September 1, 1948.

Interstate L-6, NC-48968. Licensed under the ATC for the pre-war model S1B1. At Oakland, CA, in April 1946. The hangars in the right background still have their wartime camouflage paint.

Douglas C-54A-15-DC, PI-C45, 42-72248. This Philippine Air Transport plane "Miss Mindanao" still has the AAF serial number on the fin. Photographed at Oakland Airport, CA, in June 1947.

Stinson L-5-VE, NC-66732, 42-98383. An early surplus sale photographed at Concord, CA, on October 31, 1946. There was no such thing as "warbirds" in 1946 and the demand for an L-5 was simply as a two-place private plane. Fifty years later they were considered to be a rare item for restoration in original military condition as an AAF L-5 or Navy/Marine Corps OY-1.

Stinson AT-19, Royal Navy FB756, sold as NC-67006. Five hundred of these navigation trainers were built under a U. S. Navy contract for Lend-Lease to England. At Hayward, CA, in June 1946.

Chapter 7

LIMITED TYPE CERTIFICATES

The Civil Aeronautics Administration announced in November 1946 that it had established a new Part 09 to the Civil Air Regulations to provide limited airworthiness standards for certain surplus military aircraft that were becoming available to the public, and amended Part 43 of the C.A.R. to provide for the special registration letters "NL" for such aircraft. The Board mandated that such aircraft could not be used to carry passengers or cargo for compensation or hire.

The "NL" limited airworthiness certificate was issued if there were no civilian aircraft of essentially the same basic model for which an Approved Type Certificate (ATC) had been issued and if there was no civilian counterpart model certified under the standard "NC" category.

The CAA noted specifically that "This Part is for the purpose of making available to the public certain military surplus aircraft which were originally designed for the military services of the United States...and which experience in military service has shown would be safe for operation so long as the operation is confined to flights in which neither passengers nor cargo are carried for hire."

This excerpt for the Consolidated C-87A (LTC-30) is a sample of the common statement used for all NL aircraft types. Each individual model (LTC) had an additional list of specific requirements for operating instructions in addition to deletions of certain objects or modifications to normal civilian standards.

"The aircraft may incorporate such military equipment (except armament) as was originally incorporated in the type for military or naval service. Additional equipment may be installed as can be substantiated on the basis that it presents no obvious hazard to safety.

"The following statement must appear on the Operating Limitations. 'This airplane must be operated at all times within the limitations set forth in Army Technical Order No. AN-01-50A-1 except for limitations specifically called out in Aircraft Specification AL-30 in which case the specifications must be observed. A copy of the pertinent Army Technical Order and Aircraft Specification AL-30 must be carried during flight.' In all cases it will be the responsibility of the applicant to secure copies of the Army Technical Orders. The C.A.A. does not have these documents available for distribution.

"If any repairs or modifications are made prior to and/or subsequent to NL certification, it is the responsibility of the owner to furnish sufficient evidence to a C.A.A. representative to show that the modified airplane maintains the same degree of airworthiness as the original. The C.A.A. can give no technical assistance on such matters since complete structural data for NL aircraft are not required by Part 9 and therefore are not available in the C.A.A."

The following list covers the WWII surplus types approved for a LTC with the date of issue and holder of the certificate:

LTC-1   Boeing B-17F and B-17G; December 2, 1946.
        Transcontinental and Western Air, Inc., Washington, DC.

LTC-2   North American B-25C, G, H, J and RB-25; December 6, 1946.
        Shell Aviation Corporation, New York, NY.

LTC-3   Douglas A-26B, A-26C; December 19, 1946.
        Paul V. Shields, New York, NY.

LTC-4   Douglas (Army) A-24B and (Navy) SBD-5; January 9, 1947.
        Seaboard & Western Airlines, New York City, NY.

LTC-5   Convair PB2Y-3, -3R, -5, -5R, -5Z; February 19, 1947.
        Robert M. Lewis, San Francisco, CA.

LTC-6   Convair LB-30; February 21, 1947.
        Consolidated-Vultee Aircraft Corp., San Diego, CA.

LTC-7   Sikorsky R-4B; February 28, 1947.
        Douglas W. Holmes, Compton, CA.

LTC-8   Grumman TBF-1, -1C, TBM-1, -1C, TBM-3, -3E; March 31, 1947.
        Air Trading Corporation, New York City, NY.

LTC-9   Douglas A-20B, C, G, H and J; March 31, 1947.
        Douglas Aircraft Company, Santa Monica, CA.

LTC-10 Lockheed P-38E. J (F-5E), L (F-5F/G), P-38M; April 7, 1947.
        Lockheed Aircraft Corporation, Burbank, CA.

LTC-11 North American P-51C, D, E, K; April 10, 1947.
        DePonti Aviation Company, Minneapolis, MN.

LTC-12 Beech AT-10, AT-10BH, AT-10GL and AT-10GF; April 14, 1947.
        Leland H. Cameron, Chicago, IL.

LTC-13 Lockheed B-34, PV-1, PV-2; April 15, 1947.
        Air Trading Corporation, New York City, NY.

LTC-14 Northrop P-61A, B; April 23, 1947.
        Northrop Aircraft Corporation, Hawthorne, CA.

LTC-15 North American A-36A; April 30, 1947.
        Woodrow W. Edmondson, Lynchburg, VA.

LTC-16 Curtiss O-52; May 6, 1947.
        Holmberg Aerial Survey Company, Washington, DC.

LTC-17   Grumman J2F-3, J2F-4, J2F-5, and J2F-6; May 6, 1947.
         R. B. Utterback, Long Beach, CA.

LTC-18   Curtiss P-40L, N; May 8, 1947.
         Boardman C. Reed, Pasadena, CA.

LTC-19   Sikorsky R-5A; May 15, 1947.
         Hel-I-Cop Advertising Corporation, Pasadena, CA.

LTC-20   Martin PBM-5; June 6, 1947.
         C. F. Krogmann, Washington, DC.

LTC-21   Bell P-63C, E; July 17, 1947.
         Bell Aircraft Corporation, Buffalo, NY.

LTC-22   North American BC-1; August 8, 1947.
         Mustang Aviation Inc., Dallas, TX.

LTC-23   Grumman F8F-1; August 29, 1957.
         Grumman Aircraft Corporation, Bethpage, NY.

LTC-24   Vought OS2U-1, -2, -3, and NAF OS2N-1; October 8, 1947.
         Carl F. Krogmann, Washington, DC.

LTC-25   Grumman FM-2; November 5, 1947.
         Richard R. Carlisle, Tarrant, AL.

LTC-26   Stinson L-1, A, B, C, D, E, F; November 17, 1947.
         Executive Airlines, Inc., Cleveland, OH.

LTC-27   North American BT-9, A, B, C; November 18, 1947.
         James O. Wyatt, Dyersburg, TN.

LTC-28   Culver (Superior) PQ-14A, YPQ-14A, B and TD2C-1; December 16, 1947.
         N. A. Kalt, Dallas, TX.

LTC-29   Sikorsky YR-6A, R-6A, HOS-1; January 5, 1948.
         Stolp-Adams Company, Compton, CA.

LTC-30   Convair C-87A; January 6, 1948.
         William P. Odom, Roslyn, Long Island, NY.

LTC-31   Curtiss-Wright AT-9. 9A; January 14, 1048.
         L. S. Rehr, Coral Gables, FL.

LTC-32   North American BT-14; January 14, 1948.
         P. J. Franklin, Culver City, CA.

LTC-33   Martin B-26C; July 14, 1959.
         Tennessee Gas Transmission Company, Houston, TX.

Douglas-built B-17G-85-DL, NL-3703G, 44-83546, as Tanker E-78 at Chino, CA in July 1962

North American TB-25J-35-NC, NL-66548, 45-8829. National Motor Bearing Company executive plane at San Francisco in March 1948.

Douglas A-26C-35-DT, NL-3428G, 44-35523, as Tanker T29 at Medford, Oregon in August 1966.

Consolidated LB-30, NL-1503, owned by the Continental Can Company. Currently flying as the CAF B-24 "Diamond Lil". San Francisco December 1952.

Consolidated PB2Y-5, NL-69003. at Long Beach. Purchased by Howard Hughes. (Gerald Liang)

Sikorsky R-4B, NL-75988, 43-46560, modified as a crop sprayer. At Los Angeles Central Airport in March 1948.

General Motors TBM-1C, NL-5446N, 56223, in 1947. (Logan Coombs)

Douglas A-20G-45-DO, NL-34920, 43-22197. The passenger windows of this executive modification owned by Howard Hughes can be seen at the trailing edge of the wing. San Francisco, August 1955.

Lockheed F-5G, NX-56687, 44-53183 being flown by Bill Lear, Jr., with acrobatic pilot Betty Skelton as a passenger. The number 74 was for the Bendix cross country race. Photo taken over San Francisco Bay on August 17, 1947 from the BT-13 of the Oakland Police Patrol shown in Chapter 8.

North American P-51D-10-NA, NX-33699, AAF 44-14397. Painted all black, it was flown by Joe DeBona in the Bendix Race. Photographed at Oakland in September 1947.

Lockheed-Vega PV-1, NL-64001, Navy 33317, at San Francisco in November 1955.

Beech AT-10, NL-53258, owned by the Engineering Service Company. At San Francisco in 1953.

North American A-36A, 42-83663, at the USAF Museum in Dayton, Ohio, in 1975. (Logan Coombs)

Northrop P-61B-15-NO, NX-30020, at New York in 1946. It became Tanker E53 in California. (Harold Martin)

Curtiss O-52, NL-61241, AC 40-2769, at Chicago in 1955. There were eight O-52's on the U.S. Civil Register. (Robert Stuckey)

Curtiss P-40N-5-CU, NL-1008N, 42-105878 taking off at Hayward, CA, in May 1950.

Grumman J2F-5, NL-65347, at the Dawn Patrol Seaplane Base in New York in 1948. This is a rare exception as the majority of civil Ducks are J2F-6s. (Howard Levy)

Stinson L-1E, NX-63229, on amphibious floats at Grand Central Air Terminal, Burbank, CA, on May 23, 1946.

Bell P-63C-5-BE, NX-62822, 44-4393 of Bird Airways at Long Beach, CA, in May 1946.

Martin PBM-5, NL-67903, loading lobsters at night. This was one of three PBM's with civil registrations. (Glenn L. Martin Museum)

North American BC-1. The first "AT-6" was the BC-1A derived from this fabric covered Basic Trainer. Photo at Oakland Airport in 1938.

North American BT-9C, AC No. 38-232. The standard Basic Trainer for the Army Air Corps at the time. Photographed at Oakland in 1938.

North American BT-14, NL-37604, ex-AC 40-1147. This rare fixed gear Basic Trainer, similar to the RCAF Yale, was photographed at Torrance, CA, in 1948.

Sikorsky R-6, NL-69089, modified for crop seeding. At Belmont, CA, in 1948.

Sikorsky R-6, NR-809, owned by the Asplund Tree Expert Company. (Robert Esposito)

Culver PQ-14, NX-44502. (AAF)

General Motors FM-2, Navy 86716. This clean surplus plane was at Modesto, California, in June 1947 without any N Number or indication of its new civilian ownership.

Consolidated RY-1, NL-5151N, ex-Navy 67798 and AAF C-87A 43-30570. The Reynolds-Boston Museum China Expedition plane was flown by Bill Odom.

Curtiss AT-9, 41-12025, at Mather Field, CA, in May 1942. This high performance advanced trainer was designed to train B-25 pilots. No photo has been found so far showing an AT-9 with an NL registration.

Martin B-26C, NL-171E, at San Francisco in January 1958. The executive version of the high performance B-26 had a luxurious interior. Passenger windows with curtains can be seen just ahead of the tail section.

Form ACA 331
(2-46)

UNITED STATES OF AMERICA
DEPARTMENT OF COMMERCE
CIVIL AERONAUTICS ADMINISTRATION
WASHINGTON
LIMITED AIRCRAFT

TYPE CERTIFICATE No. 18

This certificate, issued to BOARDMAN C. REED,

certifies that the following is of proper design, material, specifications, construction, and performance for safe operation, and meets the pertinent minimum standards, rules, and regulations prescribed by the Civil Aeronautics Board:

AIRCRAFT MODEL ARMY P-40N.

This certificate is of indefinite duration unless canceled, suspended, or revoked.

Date May 8, 1947

By direction of the Administrator:

(Signature) _Charles F. Dyer_
Director, Aircraft and Components Service.

This certificate may be transferred if endorsed as provided on the back hereof.

Any alteration of this certificate is punishable by a fine of not exceeding $1,000, or imprisonment not exceeding 3 years, or both.

Surplus WWII U.S. Aircraft

SERVICEABLE PLANES—LOW PRICES

Lockheed "Lodestar" Transports, Cessnas, Basic Trainers

FOR SALE

Government surplus aircraft are now available in a continuing sale through Reconstruction Finance Corporation. These models are type certificated but individual planes must be repaired to meet Civil Aeronautics Administration airworthiness requirements for civilian flight.

Lockheed "Lodestars"
Low-wing, all metal cargo and passenger transports. Powered by two Wright 1,200 h. p. engines. Hamilton standard constant-speed propellers. Gross weight: passenger, 17,500 lbs.; cargo, 18,500 lbs. Fuel capacity 644 gals. Retractable landing gear and Fowler flaps. Can be inspected at Bush Field, Augusta, Ga. Sold directly by Aircraft Division, R. F. C., 1625 K Street, N. W., Washington, D. C.
Price: $25,000 to $50,000. Can be financed.

Twin-Engine Cessnas
Powered with two Jacobs Model L4MB engines, of 225 h. p. each. Operates on 73 octane gasoline. Cruises at approximately 140 m. p. h. Low-wing wood, steel and fabric construction. For sale at all RFC Sales Centers.*
Price: $3,900 to $8,500. Can be financed.

Consolidated-Vultee Basic Trainers
Single-engine, 2-place, tandem seated, with enclosed cockpit. Powered with 450 h. p. Pratt and Whitney Wasp, Jr., and Wright engines. Equipped with dual controls and blind flying instruments. For sale at all RFC Sales Centers.*

*(SEE RFC AD PAGE 34 THIS ISSUE FOR LIST OF SALES CENTERS)

RECONSTRUCTION FINANCE CORPORATION

A DISPOSAL AGENCY DESIGNATED BY THE SURPLUS PROPERTY BOARD

AVIATION NEWS • August 20, 1945

Chapter 8

GROUP 2 (MEMO) APPROVALS

Group 2 "Letter of Approval" has a long history going back to Number 1 issued in January 1929 for an Alexander "Eaglerock" A-7. The system was designed to allow small numbers of factory production type aircraft to be licensed without undergoing the normal extensive testing for an Approved Type Certificate (ATC). In general a Group 2 Number was for a small number of slightly modified production aircraft with an engine change or addition of floats etc., but was also issued for one plane only. In all cases the approval was by factory serial number only and did not apply to any other aircraft of the same type.

However, the large numbers of World War II surplus aircraft led to a minor change, in that instead of authorizing specific manufacturers' serial numbers a blanket coverage was approved. Examples are the Douglas B-18 "All Army serial numbers" and the Douglas B-23 "All AAF Numbers."

Except for the different constructors for the modified TG-6 gliders, there were basically 13 Group 2 Approvals issued to surplus World War II aircraft.

2-544	Grumman UC-103/G32A (6-10-38)
2-548	Consolidated PBY-5A (6-24-39)
2-569	Naval Aircraft Factory N3N-3 (8-11-44)
2-570	Taylorcraft TG-6 Conversion by Commonwealth Aircraft
	2-579 by John Grosse
	2-581 by McKellar
	2-585 by W. C. King
	2-586 by Toth Flying School
	2-587 by Moberly Flying Service
	2-588 by Flight Corporation
	2-589 by Earl G. Gross
	2-590 by R. V. Black
	2-591 by Midwest Aircraft
	2-592 by Harold L. Barlow
	2-593 by Don F. Swanson
	2-594 by Louis W. Watson
	2-595 by Russel R. Carrington
	2-597 by Union Air Service
	2-598 by C. P. Grace
	2-600 by A. M. Sampson
	2-601 by V. C. Johnson
	2-602 by Edwin Little
	2-603 by William B. Eaton
	2-604 by Charles Klessig
	2-605 by Salina Aircraft
	2-606 by Leon G. Conover
	2-607 by Clark Hendrickson
	2-608 by T. Cates
	2-609 by R. F. Woolaway
2-571	Convair BT-13/15 Series (5-31-45)
2-572	North American O-47B (8-1-45)
2-473	Timm N2T-1 (11-19-45)
2-574	Canadian-Vickers Stranraer (10-15-45)
2-575	North American AT-6 Series (2-1-46)
2-576	Douglas B-23 (11-28-45)
2-577	Douglas B-18 (3-31-47)
2-578	Noorduyn Norseman UC-64
2-582	Beech AT-11, SNB-1 (5-2-46)
2-584	Culver PQ-8A, TDC-2 (5-23-46)

Grumman UC-103, N46110, 42-97045. The pre-war company plane sold surplus after World WarII service. (Leo J. Kohn)

Consolidated PBY-5A, N68740. At San Francisco in November 1953.

Chapter 8

GROUP 2 (MEMO) APPROVALS

Group 2 "Letter of Approval" has a long history going back to Number 1 issued in January 1929 for an Alexander "Eaglerock" A-7. The system was designed to allow small numbers of factory production type aircraft to be licensed without undergoing the normal extensive testing for an Approved Type Certificate (ATC). In general a Group 2 Number was for a small number of slightly modified production aircraft with an engine change or addition of floats etc., but was also issued for one plane only. In all cases the approval was by factory serial number only and did not apply to any other aircraft of the same type.

However, the large numbers of World War II surplus aircraft led to a minor change, in that instead of authorizing specific manufacturers' serial numbers a blanket coverage was approved. Examples are the Douglas B-18 "All Army serial numbers" and the Douglas B-23 "All AAF Numbers."

Except for the different constructors for the modified TG-6 gliders, there were basically 13 Group 2 Approvals issued to surplus World War II aircraft.

2-544	Grumman UC-103/G32A (6-10-38)
2-548	Consolidated PBY-5A (6-24-39)
2-569	Naval Aircraft Factory N3N-3 (8-11-44)
2-570	Taylorcraft TG-6 Conversion by Commonwealth Aircraft
	2-579 by John Grosse
	2-581 by McKellar
	2-585 by W. C. King
	2-586 by Toth Flying School
	2-587 by Moberly Flying Service
	2-588 by Flight Corporation
	2-589 by Earl G. Gross
	2-590 by R. V. Black
	2-591 by Midwest Aircraft
	2-592 by Harold L. Barlow
	2-593 by Don F. Swanson
	2-594 by Louis W. Watson
	2-595 by Russel R. Carrington
	2-597 by Union Air Service
	2-598 by C. P. Grace
	2-600 by A. M. Sampson
	2-601 by V. C. Johnson
	2-602 by Edwin Little
	2-603 by William B. Eaton
	2-604 by Charles Klessig
	2-605 by Salina Aircraft
	2-606 by Leon G. Conover
	2-607 by Clark Hendrickson
	2-608 by T. Cates
	2-609 by R. F. Woolaway
2-571	Convair BT-13/15 Series (5-31-45)
2-572	North American O-47B (8-1-45)
2-473	Timm N2T-1 (11-19-45)
2-574	Canadian-Vickers Stranraer (10-15-45)
2-575	North American AT-6 Series (2-1-46)
2-576	Douglas B-23 (11-28-45)
2-577	Douglas B-18 (3-31-47)
2-578	Noorduyn Norseman UC-64
2-582	Beech AT-11, SNB-1 (5-2-46)
2-584	Culver PQ-8A, TDC-2 (5-23-46)

Grumman UC-103, N46110, 42-97045. The pre-war company plane sold surplus after World War II service. (Leo J. Kohn)

Consolidated PBY-5A, N68740. At San Francisco in November 1953.

Naval Aircraft Factory N3N-3, NR-45086. Photo taken in May 1947 when it was operated as a rice seeder by Interstate Commercial Flyers. This early use with the original engine is less known than the more common modification with the 450 hp Wasp and other structural changes.

Canadian-Vickers Supermarine "Stranraer," NR-45327, RCAF 913, at Miami, Florida in February 1946. One of several operated by Aero Transport Corporation. (Warren M. Bodie)

Vultee BT-13B, NC-66707, operated by the Oakland Police Air Patrol. Photo at Hayward, CA, in August 1947. The air-to-air photo of Bill Lear, Jr's F-5G (see Chapter 7) was taken from this plane.

Timm N2T-1, N56520, Navy 32466, at Concord, CA in May 1954.

North American O-47A, N4725V, ex AC 38-277, in a 1954 photo. (Dustin W. Carter).

Taylorcraft DC-65, NC-62728, ex-TG-6 Glider 42-58565. There were many companies approved for this conversion and this one was done by Marston and Keyes at Hayward, California. It is being flown by AAF and USFS pilot Glenn "Red" Turner. Photographed above Hayward on May 9, 1946.

Three surplus AT-6s flying from Dos Palos to Concord, CA, on December 9, 1946. The WAA pilots flew all of these planes with the gear down as a safety measure. X-798 is AT-6B, 41-17375, from Luke Field; L-201 is AT-6A, 41-150, from Minter Field; and Z-200 is AT-6A, 41-16298, from Gila Bend AAF.

Douglas B-23, NC-67000, of the Pacific Lumber Company. At Oakland, CA, in June 1947 with a surplus BT-13 on the right.

Douglas RB-18B, N66267, AC 38-593, operated by Roberts Aircraft Company of Lovelock, Nevada, for dusting and spraying. At Reno, Nevada, in August 1952.

Noorduyn UC-64A, 43-5328, without any civil registration. It was from the Alaska Wing of the Air Transport Command. At Oakland in March 1946.

Beech AT-11, NC-62286, 42-36854, at Oakland in 1947. Several AT-11 bombardier trainers were modified as air tankers to drop retardant on forest fires. Sold to Col. Frank Kurtz of Nebraska and then to Mexico as XA-JIA.

★ ★ ★ ★ ★ ★ ★ ★ ★ ★ ★ ★ ★ ★ ★ ★ ★ ★ ★

SALE SURPLUS AIRCRAFT ENGINES

100 UNUSED PRATT & WHITNEY R-1830-75 AIRCRAFT ENGINES LOCATED DETROIT, MICHIGAN, OFFERED FOR SALE
PRICE FIXED AT $400 EACH, F.O.B., LOCATION, FOR QUICK DISPOSAL

This engine was built for the B-24N heavy bomber. The C. A. A. has certified it for use with 91 octane fuel at the maximum ratings specified for the engine regularly used in DC3 series airplanes, but the R-1830-75 engine has never actually been certified for use in any commercial airplane.

The engine has a military rating of 1350 horsepower at 2800 R.P.M., which is 150 more horsepower at take-off than the engine regularly used in DC3 airplanes. The dry weight is about 1555 pounds, approximately 90 pounds more than the regular DC3 engine. Compared with the regular DC3 engine, it has the same impeller ratio, propeller shaft ratio, propeller shaft spline and rotation.

> The WAA warrants the accuracy of the foregoing description but does not warrant, either expressed or implied, condition or the suitability of this property for any particular use. No claims for variations from warranted descriptions will be recognized unless made in writing within 15 days after the delivery to the purchaser at the storage point.

PRIORITY TIME TABLE

1st Priority: Federal Government Agencies—October 2, 1946
2nd Priority: Veterans of World War II—October 3, 1946 through October 17, 1946
3rd Priority: R.F.C. for resale to small business—October 18, 1946
4th Priority: State and Local Governments—October 19, 1946

These engines will be available for sale to the general public (non-priority groups) after October 19, 1946

Those who desire to exercise their preference must present a valid Veterans' Preference Certificate prior to purchase. (Consult the nearest WAA Regional or District Office for information as to where Veterans' Certification may be obtained.)

HOW TO BUY

Checks made payable to Treasurer of United States must accompany order. Mail order to War Assets Administration, Office of Aircraft Disposal, 425 Second Street, N.W., Washington 25, D. C.

WAR ASSETS ADMINISTRATION

ADDRESS ALL INQUIRIES TO: OFFICE OF AIRCRAFT DISPOSAL, WAR ASSETS ADMINISTRATION, 425 SECOND STREET, N.W., WASHINGTON 25, D. C.

★ ★ ★ ★ ★ ★ ★ ★ ★ ★ ★ ★ ★ ★ ★ ★ ★ ★ ★

Chapter 9

RESTRICTED AND EXPERIMENTAL CERTIFICATES

The use of the letter "R" for Restricted on aircraft registration marks goes back to the 1930's and was used for special purpose aircraft such as crop dusting. At that time it was allocated to a single airplane. The postwar influx of numbers of surplus military aircraft of the same type made this system inefficient so a temporary Restricted Certificate for certain types of aircraft was instituted. This allowed the licensing of more than one aircraft of the same type for the same purpose without individual inspection. The official CAA statement was "An aircraft of the subject series is considered eligible for restricted airworthiness certification when modified for a special purpose in accordance with Part 8 of the Civil Air Regulations." World War II NR aircraft were used for crop dusting, aerial photography, surveying, aerial advertising and other special or industrial uses.

A more detailed explanation of the Restricted Category is shown in the following excerpts from CAA Regulations:

"Any aircraft of the following classifications shall be issued a type certificate in the restricted category, if the Administrator finds that no feature or characteristic of the aircraft renders it unsafe when operated in accordance with the limitations prescribed for its intended use. 1) An aircraft type which has not previously been type certificated but which is shown by the applicant to comply with all of the airworthiness requirements of any other aircraft category prescribed by the Civil Air Regulations, except those requirements which the Administrator finds inappropriate for the special purpose for which the aircraft is to be used, or 2) An aircraft type which has been manufactured in accordance with the requirements of, and accepted for use by, a United States military service and subsequently modified for a special purpose. Whether or not such aircraft has been issued a type certificate under the provisions of the Civil Air Regulations."

"A modification of a type certificated may be issued to an applicant for an aircraft which has previously been type certificated in another category and then modified for a special pupose when, upon inspection, the Administrator finds that the modifications conform to a good aeronautical practice and that no feature or characteristic of the aircraft renders it unsafe when operated in accordance with the limitations prescribed for its intended use."

"In addition to the operating limitations set forth in 8.31 through 8.34 the Administrator shall prescribe such operating limitations and restric-

tions as he finds necessary for safe operation of the aircraft and for the protection of the public. Special purpose operations in restricted category aircraft shall not be conducted over densely populated areas, in congested air lanes, or in the vicinity of busy airports where passenger transport operations are being conducted, unless the Administrator finds it in the public interest to allow operations in such areas, in which case he shall prescribe specific operating limitations to provide the highest degree of public safety compatible with the type of operations involved. Persons and cargo shall not be carried for compensation or hire in restricted category aircraft. For purposes of this section crop dusting, seeding, and other similar specialized operations, including the carriage of material necessary for such operations, shall not be considered as the carriage of persons or cargo for compensation or hire. Persons, other than the minimum crew necessary for the purpose involved, shall not be carried during special purpose operations in restricted category aircraft."

It is unclear when the new AR (Aircraft Restricted) classification started. The dates on all of the original documents are in the 1950's as shown in the following list which for the purposes of this book is limited to World War II aircraft. If this is correct ,it started with AR-1 in May 1951. All of the AR's carried this statement: "For special purpose operations over congested areas, the military operating limitations must be submitted by the applicant for the use of the CAA representative in establishing civil limitations in accordance with Civil Air Regulations Part 8.30."

AR-1 Curtiss-Wright Army P-40 Series; May 21, 1951.
      Rogue River Valley Traffic Association, Medford, OR.

AR-2 Naval Aircraft Factory N3N-1; July 9, 1951. Crowl Dusters, Phoenix, AZ.

AR-3 Federal XPT-1; July 23, 1951.
      Wilson Air Service, Bridgeton, NY.

AR-4 DeHavilland Mosquito (Army F-8); (Date unknown)
      An April 15, 1955 Revision 1 states "Type Certificate No. AR-4 was cancelled on this date at the request of the type certificate holder. No additional aircraft of this model are eligible for original certification under this type certificate."

AR-5 Avro Anson V; January 9, 1952.
      Continental Oil Company, Ponca City, OK.

AR-6 St. Louis YPT-15; February 5, 1952.
      Arizona Aviation Service, Stafford, AZ.

AR-9 Stearman 73 (Navy NS-1); June 4, 1952.
      Southwest Aircraft Inc., Fort Worth, TX. (Not Shown)

AR-11 Noorduyn Harvard (Army AT-16); January 12, 1955.
      Autair Ltd., London, England

AR-12 Northrop RF-61C, RF-15; May 13, 1955.
      Steward-Davis, Inc., Gardena, CA. (Not Shown)

AR-13 DeHavilland Mosquito (Army F-8); June 10, 1955.
      Trans World Engineering Corp., Los Angeles, CA. (Not Shown)

AR-15 Fairchild C-82; July 7, 1955.
      Steward-Davis, Inc., Gardena, CA.

AR-18 Grumman F6F; September 28, 1955.
      Thomas Jennings, Washington, DC.

AR-19 Curtiss SB2C; October 12, 1955.
      Clayton V. Curtiss, Visalia, CA

AR-22 Convair PBY-6A; July 2, 1956.
      The Babb Company, Inc., Phoenix, AZ.

AR-23 Seversky P-35; March 5, 1957.
      Charles P. Doyle, Rosemount, MN.

AR-24 Boeing YC-97; April 9, 1957.
DeLong Corporation. New York City, NY
(Photo on page 114).

There is some confusion over individual planes of these types being issued an Experimental Certificate as shown in several of the photos in this Chapter. The explanation is most likely that a number of modifications were made to the plane so that it no longer met the specifications for the Restricted category. In general, World War II production aircraft could be certified under any of the three categories, NL, NR, NX, depending upon the purpose for which they were used. During the immediate postwar period NX Experimental was often used for exhibition and air racing purposes.

AR-1 Curtiss P-40E, NR-1223N, RCAF 1038, at Oakland, CA in 1955. It was operated by Weather Modification Company for four years as a rain maker — seeding clouds at 20,000 feet with silver iodide. Six former RCAF P-40Es got U.S. civil registrations.

AR-2 Naval Aircraft Factory XN3N-1, Navy 9991, at the surplus sales area of Westchester County Airport, New York, in August 1945. The enclosed canopy was a late addition to the XN3N-1.

AR-3 Federal XPT, NX-1280, at Roosevelt Field in New York in 1939. It was a crop duster in Florida in 1965. (Howard Levy)

AR-4 DeHavilland Mosquito, N9909F, at Whitman Air Park in Los Angeles. (Lee Enich)

AR-5 Federal Aircraft of Canada-built Avro "Anson" used by the AAF as the AT-20. This is a wartime photo of 43-8215 at Keesler Field, Biloxi, Mississippi. (AAF)

AR-6 St. Louis YPT-15, N67328, as modified in Arizona in the 1960s. (Brian Baker)

AR-8 Douglas A-24B-10-DT, 42-54582, used by the City of Portland for Mosquito Control. The plane is now in the Marine Corps Museum as an SBD-5. Photo at Troutdale, Oregon, in August 1966.

AR-11 Noorduyn Harvard II, RCAF AJ832, at Merced, CA in June 1965. Built in Canada, this is the same type of aircraft as the AAF AT-16.

AR-15 Fairchild C-82A-20-FA, 44-23026, modified and operated as a sprayer by United Heckathorn of Richmond, CA, who had five of these. N4832V is shown at Hayward, CA, in May 1956.

AR-18 Grumman F6F-3, N4965V, USN 08825, at Hayward, CA in October 1955.

AR-19 Curtiss RA-25A, NX-67858, at Santa Monica, CA, in June 1947. The Douglas factory is in the left background. It was being flown as part of the Wilson King Sky Shows. (Henry Arnold)

AR-22 Consolidated PBY-6A, N6681C, Navy 64092. Its last duty was with the Naval Reserve at Atlanta, Georgia, and it shows a typical hand painted N Number. Location and date unknown. (Larkins Collection)

AR-23 Republic AT-12, NX-55811, 41-17513. The two-seat training version of the P-35 photographed at Cleveland, Ohio, during the National Air Races in September 1946. (Warren Bodie)

Bell P-39Q-20-BE, NX-4829N, 44-3908, at Concord, CA, in January 1955. It was later re-registered as N40A.

Curtiss SNC-1, NX-19446, modified for the 1949 National Air Races. It was entered by Jane Page in the Halle Trophy Race but withdrawn after severe criticism because all of the other planes were AT-6s. Photo at Cleveland, Ohio, on September 2, 1949. (Lawrence S. Smalley)

North American P-51A, NX-33648, 43-6007, at Clover Field, Santa Monica, CA, in October 1948. Another surplus P-51A can be seen in the background under the engine.

Curtiss P-36A, N52203. A rare civil registered Army Air Corps fighter of the 1930s. (Robert Stuckey)

Fairchild AT-21, NX-63432, at Vail Field, Los Angeles, in May 1946. At least ten of these were on the U. S. Civil Register by 1949.

Curtiss SO3C-1, NX-41806, flown by the Ranger Aircraft Engine Company. (Larkins Collection)

North American P-64, NX-37498, 41-19085, when it was being operated as a rain maker at Phoenix, Arizona, in May 1948. It went to Mexico as XB-KUU and returned to the U.S. to be purchased by the Experimental Aircraft Association where it is now a museum exhibit.

Surplus WWII U.S. Aircraft

USED TRAINING PLANES
FOR SALE $875 TO $2400

SINGLE-ENGINE PRIMARY TRAINER AIRPLANES
GOVERNMENT SURPLUS PROPERTY
AVAILABLE THROUGH RECONSTRUCTION FINANCE CORPORATION

TYPES AVAILABLE:
Fairchild Army Models PT-19, PT-23; Boeing Army Models PT-17, PT-27; Navy Models N2S-1, N2S-3, N2S-4; Ryan PT-22; and Naval Aircraft Factory N3N-3.

These planes can be used for flight instruction, personal transportation, crop dusting, ranch or forest patrol and other purposes.

They are powered with in-line or radial type engines ranging from 160 to 235 horsepower, and are two-place, tandem, open cockpit monoplanes or biplanes of composite construction. These models are type-certificated but individual planes must be repaired to meet Civil Aeronautics Administration airworthiness requirements for civilian flight.

All of the above types formerly were used by the Army and Navy in their respective pilot training programs.

Information on sales procedure, location of available aircraft, and selling prices may be obtained from your nearest RFC Disposing Agency.

RECONSTRUCTION FINANCE CORPORATION
A DISPOSAL AGENCY DESIGNATED BY THE SURPLUS PROPERTY BOARD

Agencies located at: Atlanta • Boston • Charlotte • Chicago • Cleveland • Dallas • Denver • Detroit Houston • Kansas City, Mo. • Los Angeles • Minneapolis • New Orleans • New York • Omaha • Philadelphia • Portland, Ore. • Richmond • St. Louis • Salt Lake City • San Antonio • San Francisco • Seattle

BUY WAR BONDS

APPENDICES

1: World War II Surplus Aircraft Storage, Sales and Salvage Yards

2: Storage and Sales Depots

3: WAA Distribution of Aircraft Inventory

4: WAA Sales and Salvage Aircraft by Type

5: WAA Sales and Salvage Total by Class

6: Price List for Tactical Aircraft – 1946

7: Price List for Non-Tactical Aircraft

8: Transport Aircraft Prices

9: Civil Aircraft Sales

10: AAF Impressed Civil Aircraft Declared Surplus

11: Vultee BT Aircraft For Sale

12: FAA Aircraft Codes

13: CAA Aircraft Totals For 1947

14: Additional CAA Aircraft Totals For 1949

SPARE ENGINES for BT-13 and C-45 OWNERS

Used, repairs required

PRATT & WHITNEY "WASP, JR."

450 HP (ONE DOLLAR PER HORSE POWER)

Located at Harvey Park Airport, Sikeston, Mo.
Models R-985-AN1 and R-985-AN3

Three hundred thirty surplus used Pratt & Whitney "Wasp, Jr.", 450 horsepower aircraft engines now located at Sikeston, Mo. Were originally installed in BT-13's when they were flown into Sikeston. Can be adapted for use in Beech C-45's. To be sold on an "as is, first come, first served basis." Prospective customers may inspect before buying. Many engines are equipped with generators, starters, magnetos and carburetors, although War Assets Administration cannot make any warranty as to condition of accessories or availability thereof. It is only necessary to present your check payable to Treasurer, United States, to Harvey Park Airport.

USED, REPAIRS REQUIRED

OTHER "WASP JR." ENGINES LOCATED AT VARIOUS OTHER PLACES

	Price
Unused	$3,912
Used, Reconditioned	3,179
Used, Usable Without Repairs	560
Used, Repairs Required	450

NOTE: May also be used on the following plane models: AT-7, AT11, BT12, C43, C70, F2 & R5.

No warranties are given as to condition or serviceability.

$450 Ea. FOB Location used, repairs required

WRITE FOR FULL INFORMATION
Address all inquiries to:
AIRCRAFT DIVISION

WAR ASSETS ADMINISTRATION

425 Second Street, N.W., Washington 25, D.C.

VETERANS OF WORLD WAR II: This surplus property is offered to priority claimants, including veterans of World War II.

489

GOVERNMENT SURPLUS AIRCRAFT

CONSOLIDATED-VULTEE BASIC TRAINERS

FOR SALE by RFC at

$975

less 20% reduction on purchase of three or more at one time by one person*—with ferrying allowance of 27¢ per mile not to exceed $90 a plane.

UNTIL MARCH 16, 1946

Single-engine, 2-place, tandem seated, with enclosed cockpit. Powered with 450 h.p. Pratt & Whitney Wasp, Jr., and Wright engines. Equipped with dual controls and blind flying instruments. Type certificated by the Civil Aeronautics Administration and are eligible for airworthiness certificates upon completion of all necessary repairs and modifications required by the CAA.

For sale until March 16, 1946, at RFC Storage Depots. If you do not know the most convenient depot, consult the nearest agency listed below. Ask for the aircraft representative.

* *If you have previously qualified for the 20% reduction, this 20% applies to purchase of a single plane.*

VETERANS...

To help you in purchasing surplus property from the RFC, a veterans' unit has been established in each of our Disposing Agencies.

RECONSTRUCTION FINANCE CORPORATION

A Disposal Agency Designated by the Surplus Property Administration

Agencies located at: Atlanta • Birmingham • Boston • Charlotte • Chicago
Cleveland • Dallas • Denver • Detroit • Helena • Houston • Jacksonville
Kansas City, Mo. • Little Rock • Los Angeles • Louisville • Minneapolis
Nashville • New Orleans • New York • Oklahoma City • Omaha • Philadelphia
Portland, Ore. • Richmond • St. Louis • Salt Lake City • San Antonio
San Francisco • Seattle • Spokane

2

Appendix 1

WORLD WAR II SURPLUS AIRCRAFT STORAGE, SALES AND SALVAGE YARDS

City	*Airport/Field*	*Remarks*
Birmingham, AL	Municipal Airport	RFC Sales
Decatur, AL	Municipal Airport	RFC, WAA
Mobile, AL	Brookley Field	AAF Storage
Pine Bluff, AR	Grider Field	RFC, WAA
Walnut Ridge, AR	Walnut Ridge AAF	WAA
West Helena, AR	Thompson-Robbins Field	RFC
Kingman, AZ	Kingman Army Air Field	WAA
Phoenix, AZ	NAF Litchfield Park	USN
Phoenix, AZ	Thunderbird Field II	RFC, WAA
Tucson, AZ	Davis-Monthan Field	AAF Storage
Tucson, AZ	Ryan Field	RFC, WAA
Wickenburg, AZ	Echeverria Field	RFC, WAA
Alameda, CA	NAS Alameda	Storage & Salvage
Blythe, CA	Gary Field	RFC, WAA
Burbank, CA	Lockheed Air Terminal	RFC
Concord, CA	Sherman Field	RFC
Concord, CA	Buchanan Field	WAA
Dos Palos, CA	Eagle Field	RFC, WAA
Fresno, CA	Chandler Field	RFC
Hemet, CA	Ryan Field	RFC
Ontario, CA	Cal-Aero Field	RFC, WAA
Sacramento, CA	McClellan Field	AAF Storage
San Bernardino, CA	San Bernardino AAF	AAF Storage
San Diego, CA	NAS San Diego	Storage & Salvage
San Jose, CA	San Jose Airport	RFC
Victorville, CA	Victorville AAF	AAF Storage
Denver, CO	Hayden Field	RFC
Dupont, CO	Rutledge Field	RFC
Simsbury, CT	Simsbury Airport	RFC
Dover, DE	Dover Airport	RFC
Jacksonville, FL	NAS Jacksonville	Storage & Salvage
Miami, FL	Chapman Field	RFC
Miami, FL	NAS Miami	Salvage
St. Petersburg, FL	Ludwig Sky Harbor	RFC

Americus, GA	Souther Field	RFC, WAA
Augusta, GA	Bush Field	RFC, WAA
Douglas, GA	Municipal Airport	RFC
Warner-Robbins, GA	Robbins Field	AAF Storage
Lansing, IL	Ford-Lansing Airport	RFC
Indianapolis, IN	Sky Harbor Airport	RFC
Davenport, IA	Cran Field	RFC
Des Moines, IA	Municipal Airport	RFC
Garden City, KS	Garden City AAF	AAF Storage
Independence, KS	Independence AAF	AAF Storage
Wichita, KS	Municipal Airport	RFC
Baton Rouge, LA	East Baton Rouge Parish	RFC
North Grafton, MA	North Grafton Airport	RFC
Lansing, MI	Capitol City Airport	RFC
Minneapolis, MN	Victory Airport	RFC
Clarksdale, MS	Fletcher Field	RFC
Greenville, MS	Greenville AAF	AAF Storage
Grenada, MS	Grenada AAF	AAF Storage
Laurel, MS	Laurel AAF	AAF Storage
Madison, MS	Augustine Field	RFC, WAA
Cape Girardeau, MO	Harris Field	RFC, WAA
Kansas City, MO	Municipal Airport	RFC
Robertson, MO	Municipal Airport	RFC
Sikeston, MO	Harvey Park Airport	RFC
Great Falls, MT	Gore Field	RFC
Helena, MT	Municipal Airport	RFC
Omaha, NB	Municipal Airport	RFC
Reno, NV	Reno Sky Ranch	RFC
Newark NJ	Newark AAF	AAF Storage
Readington, NJ	Solberg-Hunterton Airport	RFC
Albuquerque, NM	West Mesa Airport	RFC
Albuquerque, NM	Albuquerque AAF	WAA

Hobbs, NM	Hobbs AAF	AAF Storage
Albany, NY	Albany Airport	RFC
Rochester, NY	Municipal Airport	RFC
Rome, NY	Rome AAF	AAF Storage
Syracuse, NY	Syracuse AAF	AAF Storage
White Plains, NY	Westchester County Airport	RFC
Charlotte, NC	Cannon Field	RFC
Akron, OH	Municipal Airport	RFC
Cincinnati, OH	Lunken Field	RFC
Dayton, OH	Patterson Field	AAF Storage & Salvage
Altus, OK	Altus AAF	WAA
Clinton, OK	NAS Clinton	USN, WAA
El Reno, OK	Mustang Field	RFC
Muskogee, OK	Hat Box Field	RFC, WAA
Oklahoma City, OK	Cimarron Field	RFC, WAA
Oklahoma City, OK	Tinker Field	AAF Storage
Ponca City, OK	Municipal Airport	RFC, WAA
Stillwater, OK	Municipal Airport	RFC
Portland, OR	Portland-Troutdale Airport	RFC
Collegeville, PA	Perkiomen Valley Airport	RFC
Montoursville, PA	Williamsport Airport	RFC
Pittsburgh, PA	Bettis Field	RFC
Bennettsville, SC	Palmer Field	RFC
Camden, SC	Woodward Field	RFC, WAA
Huron, SD	Municipal Airport	RFC
Sioux Falls, SD	Sioux Field	RFC
Jackson, TN	McKellar Field	RFC, WAA
Union City, TN	Embry-Riddle Field	RFC, WAA
Ballinger, TX	Bruce Field	RFC, WAA
Corsicana, TX	Corsicana Airport	RFC
Cuero, TX	Municipal Airport	RFC, WAA
Fort Stockton, TX	Gibbs Field	RFC, WAA
Fort Worth, TX	Hicks Field	RFC, WAA
Houston, TX	Municipal Airport	RFC
Lamesa, TX	Lamesa Airport	RFC, WAA
Lubbock, TX	South Plains AAF	AAF Storage
Pyote, TX	Pyote AAF	AAF Storage
San Antonio, TX	Municipal Airport	RFC
San Antonio, TX	Kelly Field	AAF Storage

Stamford, TX	Ariedge Field	RFC, WAA
Vernon, TX	Victory Field	RFC, WAA
Ogden, UT	Hill Field	AAF Storage
Salt Lake City, UT	Municipal Airport No. 1	RFC
Alexandria, VA	Hybla Valley Airport	RFC
Norfolk, VA	NAS Norfolk	USN, WAA
Olympia, WA	Olympia AAF	RFC
Spokane, WA	Calkins Field	RFC
Morgantown, WV	Municipal Airport	RFC

Appendix 2

STORAGE AND SALES DEPOTS

I. DEFENSE PLANT CORPORATION STORAGE DEPOTS
    Embry-Riddle Field, Union City, Tennessee
    McKeller Field, Jackson, Tennessee
    Fletcher Field, Clarksdale, Mississippi
    Woodward Field, Camden, South Carolina
    Palmer Field, Bennetsville, South Carolina
    Victory Field, Vernon, Texas
    Ponce City Municipal Airport, Ponce City, Oklahoma
    Harvey Parks Airport, Sikeston, Missouri
    Ryan Field, Tucson, Arizona
    Gary Field, Blythe, California
    Lamesa Field, Lamesa, Texas
    Bruce Field, Ballinger, Texas
    Stanford Field, Stanford, Texas
    Gibbs Field, Fort Stockton, Texas
    Thompson-Robbins Field, West Helena, Arkansas
    Cuero Municipal Airport, Cuero, Texas

II. SALES STORAGE DEPOTS
    Augustine Field, Madison, Mississippi
    Bush Field, Augusta, Georgia
    Southern Field, Americus, Georgia
    Cimarron Field, Oklahoma City, Oklahoma
    Hat Box Field, Muskogee, Oklahoma
    Harris Field, Cape Girardeau, Missouri
    Cal-Aero Field, Ontario, California
    Echeverria Field, Wickenburg, Arizona
    Thunderbird II Field, Phoenix, Arizona
    Hicks Field, Fort Worth, Texas
    Grider Field, Pine Bluff, Arkansas

III. RECONSTRUCTION FINANCE CORPORATION SALES CENTERS
    Akron Airways, Municipal Airport, Akron, Ohio
    Albany Aircraft Company, Albany Airport, Albany, New York
    Ashburn Flying Service, Hybla Valley Airport, Alexandria, Virginia
    Bettis Airport, Pittsburg, Pennsylvania
    Aviation Activities Company, Concord, California.
    Aviation Enterprises Ltd., Municipal Airport, Houston, Texas
    Brayton Flying Service, Municipal Airport, Robertson, Missouri
    Cannon Aircraft Sales & Service, Cannon Airport, Charlotte, North Carolina
    Central Aviation Corp., Municipal Airport, Omaha, Nebraska

Cincinnati Air Service, Lunken Airport, Cincinnati, Ohio
Cutter-Carr Flying Service, West Mesa Airport, Albuquerque, New Mexico
Dakota Aviation Company, Municipal Airport, Huron, South Dakota
Des Moines Flying Service, Municipal Airport, Des Moines, Iowa
Great Plains Aviation, Rutledge Airport, Dupont, Colorado
Harte Flying Service, Municipal Airport, Wichita, Kansas
Hilsen Area Service, Calkins Airport, Spokane, Washington
Hughes Flying Service, Capitol City Airport, Lansing, Michigan
Jennings Brothers Air Service, North Grafton Airport, North Grafton, Massachusetts
Clarence Ludwig, Ludwig Sky Harbor, St. Petersburg, Florida
Frysdale Flying Service, Victory Airport, Minneapolis, Minnesota
Morrison Flying Service, Municipal Airport, Helena, Montana
Robert Slamp Flying Service, Fort Lansing Airport, Lansing, Illinois
Thor Solberg, Solberg-Hunterton Airport, Readington, New Jersey
Thompson Flying Service, Municipal Airport No. 2, Salt Lake City, Utah

Appendix 3

WAA DISTRIBUTION OF AIRCRAFT INVENTORY

The Inventory of surplus aircraft located at War Assets Corporation Sales Centers and Sales Storage Depots as of January 24, 1946. The order of aircraft is as listed by the WAC.

ALBUQUERQUE, NEW MEXICO
5 PT-19, 23 BT-13, 246 AT-6, 8 C-78, 1 AT-17, 13 TG-6, 2 A-20, 3 A-24, 175 B-17, 264 B-24, 30 B-25, 2 B-26, 104 P-39, 641 P-40, 304 P-47, 57 P-51, 3 P-64, 99 PB4Y, 1 A-23, 6 A-36, 1 F-5, 2 F-7, 1 F-10, 1 R-37, 1 TG-31.

ALTUS, OKLAHOMA
2 AT-6, 1 C-78, 17 A-20, 7 A-24, 603 B-17, 1272 B-24, 341 B-25, 145 B-26, 2 B-32, 1 B-40, 112 P-38, 1 P-39, 50 P-40, 42 P-47, 1 P-51, 5 P-63, 7 PB4Y, 1 TBF-1, 1 A-36.

AMERICUS, GEORGIA
106 BT-13, 106 AT-6, 1 BC-1A, 7 C-78, 18 TG-5, 50 TG-32, 2 TG-2, 1 A-17, 1 A-24, 2 AT-10, 1 C-76, 1 R-37, 21 CG-3, 21 TG-3.

AUGUSTA, GEORGIA
1 L-5, 5 PT-17, 1 PT-19, 2 N2S-1, 190 BT-13, 16 BT-15, 2 SNV-1, 12 AT-6, 15 AT-11, 6 BC-1A, 21 C-47, 4 C-49, 9 C-53, 32 C-54, 1 C-59, 45 C-60, 18 C-64, 31 C-78, 1 F-2, 22 B-18, 1 O-47, 22 AT-21, 1 A-17, 1 A-19, 80 A-20, 176 A-24, 51 A-25, 1 A-33, 36 B-17, 64 B-24, 2 B-25, 30 B-26, 33 B-34, 4 P-38, 35 P-39, 126 P-40, 1 P-43, 44 P-47, 25 P-61, 1 P-64, 1 OA-12, 1 F4F- 4, J2F, 9 J2F-6, 14 OS2U, 1 PB4Y, 1 SB2A, 2 TBM-1, 5 TBF-1, 83 C-46, 1 BT-9, 5 BT-14, 10 AT-9, 103 AT-10, 1 AT-16, 40 AT-18, 1 O-38, 30 C-87, 12 A-29, 4 A-35, 13 A-36, 13 F-6, 3 F-7, 1 F-9, 1 P-70, 5 P-322, 34 B-37, 1 SB2C, 1 YG-13, 1 PQ-14.

BALLINGER, TEXAS
2 PT-13, 79 BT-13, 256 SNV-1, 32 C-78, 215 AT-10.

BLYTHE, CALIFORNIA
10 PT-13, 17 PT-17, 8 PT-27, 342 BT-13, 84 C-78, 87 AT-17, 4 O-47, 1 A-25, 2 B-37, 15 AT-9, 8 AT-10.

CAMDEN, SOUTH CAROLINA
20 L-4, 5 L-5, 2 NE-1, 15 PT-13, 57 PT-17, 12 N2S-4, 1 N3N-3, 171 BT-13, 10 SNV-1, 164 AT-6, 2 BC-1A, 3 C-64, 34 C-78, 2 AT-17, 1 JRC-1, 20 A-24, 2 A-25, 193 AT-10, 1 J4F-2, 1 A-35.

CAPE GIRADEAU, MISSOURI
434 PT-23, 8 N2S-1, 40 N3N-3, 136 N2T-1, 31 C-78, 12 AT-17, 4 A-25. 37 AT-10.

CLARKSDALE, MISSISSIPPI
2 PT-17, 5 PT-19, 1 BT-13, 3 C-78.

CLINTON, OKLAHOMA
1 N2S-2, 227 N2S-4, 363 SNV-1, 170 SNV-2, 1 F4F, 1382 FM-2, 413 F4U-1, 368 FG-1, 1151 F6F, 30 OS2U-2, 136 OS2U-3, 145 PB4Y, 3 SO3C-1, 580 TBM-1, 369 TBF-1, 237 AT-10, 4 AT-18, 107 F-3, 55 OS2N, 1 PBY-5A, 268 PV-1, 10 PV-3, 327 PBJ-1, 2 SB2C, 3 SBD-3, 615 SBD-5, 79 SBD-6, 1 SBN-1, 72 SBF-3, 70 SBW-3, 2 TBM-3.

CUERO, TEXAS
65 BT-13, 2 AT-11, 330 C-78, 92 AT-17, 2 A-24.

DECATUR, ALABAMA
142 PT-17, 329 BT-13, 86 SNV-2.

DOS PALOS, CALIFORNIA
29 L-5, 133 PT-17, 3 PT-22, 283 BT-13, 7 SNV-2, 50 AT-6, 1 C-60, 1 C-64, 1 C-78.

EL RENO, OKLAHOMA
76 PT-17, 485 BT-13.

FT. STOCKTON, TEXAS
1 PT-13, 2 PT-17, 127 BT-13, 404 BT-15, 3 C-78, 56 AT-10.

FT. WORTH, TEXAS
1 L-2, 3 L-3, 1 L-4, 1 PT-27, 264 PT-13, 75 C-78, 102 AT-17, 7 TG-1, 55 TG-5, 1 TG-6, 2 A-24.

HARVEY POINT, NORTH CAROLINA
100 PBM, 5 PB2B, 7 PBY-5, 4 PBY-5A.

JACKSON, TENNESSEE
1 J-5, 1 PT-17, 1 PT-19, 1 PT-22, 2 N2S-1, 27 N2S-3, 265 BT-13, 24 BT-15, 45 AT-6, 27 BC-1A, 73 C-78, 50 B-18, 40 O-47, 1 AT-12, 27 A-17, 2 A-20, 28 A-24, 2 A-25, 2 A-33, 7 B-25, 5 B-34, 1 P-36, 37 P-40, 11 P-47, 5 0-46, 2 SB2A, 6 BT-9, 1 BT-12, 192 AT-10, 2 A-29, 1 B-23, 12 R-37.

KINGMAN, ARIZONA
1 BT-13, 13 AT-6, 51 A-20, 27 A-26, 1699 B-17, 2396 B-24, 64 B-25, 80 B-26, 35 B-32, 438 P-38, 10 P-40, 30 P-47, 119 P-63, 3 C-87, 2 C-109, 6 B-30, 60 F-5.

LAMESA, TEXAS
1 PT-19, 11 PT-27, 370 BT-13, 30 C-78, 30 AT-17, 27 AT-18, 31 TG-3.

MADISON, MISSISSIPPI
11 PT-17, 37 PT-19, 20 BT-13, 139 C-78, 57 AT-17, 8 A-24, 130 AT-10.

MUSKEGEE, OKLAHOMA
6 L-4, 38 L-5, 10 BT-13, 15 BC-1A, 1 B-18, 4 A-20, 17 A-24, 19 A-25, 7 A-28, 1 A-33, 3 B-26, 33 B-34, 1 P-39, 328 AT-9, 56 AT-19, 2 A-29, 1 P-322, 31 R-37.

OKLAHOMA CITY, OKLAHOMA
1 N2S-2, 5 N3N-3, 32 BT-13, 3 BT-15, 1 BC-1A, 1 C-64, 287 C-78, 73 TG-6, 38 O-52, 2 BT-9, 1 AT-10, 10 TG-3.

ONTARIO, CALIFORNIA
1 J-5, 1 PT-17, 50 BT-13, 173 AT-6, 4 C-47, 1 C-60, 246 C-78, 7 AT-17, 2 JRC-1, 11 TG-5, 1 TG-6, 2 B-18, 1 O-47, 109 A-20, 86 A-24, 12 A-25, 80 B-17, 241 B-24, 22 B-25, 126 B-26, 3 B-34, 4 B-37, 197 P-38, 237 P-39, 71 P-40, 1 P-43, 40 P-47, 3 P-61, 10 P-400, 1 J2F-6, 11 PB4Y, 33 C-46, 18 AT-10, 1 AT-18, 6 J2F-5, 13 A-29, 7 A-36, 1 FM-2, 1 PBY-5A.

PHOENIX, ARIZONA
4 PT-17. 1 PT-27. 27 BT-13, 92 C-78, 23 TG-5, 1 TBF-1.

PINE BLUFF, ARKANSAS
5 N2S-2, 13 BT-13, 11 BT-15, 121 SNV-1, 37 C-78, 78 AT-17, 190 AT-10.

PONCA CITY, OKLAHOMA
1 L-4, 1 PT-17, 3 PT-19, 2 N2S-2, 4 N3N-3, 119 BT-13, 4 BT-15, 4 SNV-2, 154 AT-6, 1 AT-7, 139 AT-11, 1 C-32, 1 C-64, 4 C-78. 1 JRC-1, 125 AT-21, 1 A-20, 23 A-24, 5 A-25, 95 B-25, 10 P-39, 35 P-40, 16 P-47, 2 P-51, 7 AT-9, 2 AT-10, 1 AT-18, 5 SBD-4.

SIKESTON, MISSOURI
3 PT-23, 4 N2S-1, 1 BT-13, 25 SNV-1, 1 A-24, 1 A-25, 7 B-34, 2 B-37, 1 BT-9, 2 BT-14, 58 AT-10, 30 AT-18, 3 A-36.

STAMFORD, TEXAS
1 N2S-2, 74 BT-13, 1 C-78, 148 AT-17, 1 B-18, 6 AT-21, 1 A-20, 7 A-24, 1 A-25, 12 B-17, 1 B-24, 6 B-34, 7 B-37, 4 P-39, 16 P-40, 1 P-47, 1 BT-9, 2 BT-14, 58 AT-10, 30 AT-18, 3 A-36.

STILLWATER, OKLAHOMA
1 B-18, 1 A-20, 78 B-17, 145 B-24, 10 B-25, 22 B-26, 6 P-39, 90 P-40, 31 P-47, 7 P-51, 8 PB4Y, 2 F-7.

Tucson, Arizona
5 PT-17, 19 BT-13, 1 BC-1A, 79 C-78,
40 AT-17, 2 B-18, 1 C-47, 2 A-24, 1 A-25,
1 AT-10.

Union City, Texas
1 PT-19, 444 PT-23, 268 BT-13, 158 SNV-1,
8 C-78, 2 AT-17, 2 A-24, 1 A-25, 380 AT-10.

Vernon, Texas
2 PT-19, 3 N2S-1, 2 N2S-2, 118 N2S-4,
431 BT-13, 20 SNV-1, 75 SNV-2, 1 BC-1A,
66 C-78, 122 AT-17, 1 JRC-1, 5 A-24,
1 A-25, 7 P-47, 16 AT-9, 55 AT-10, 1 AT-18.

Walnut Ridge, Arkansas
7 BT-13, 167 BT-15, 1 AT-6, 191 C-47,
85 C-54, 2 C-60, 2 C-64, 28 A-20, 6 A-24,
1 A-25, 1 A-26, 1211 B-17, 1148 B-24,
513 B-25, 261 B-26, 67 B-32, 8 B-40,
100 P-38, 1 P-39, 462 P-40, 346 P-47,
102 P-51, 152 P-63, 10 PB4Y, 369 C-46,
38 AT-10, 1 AT-24, 7 C-87, 1 A-29, 4 A-36,
7 B-30, 5 F-3, 1 F-7, 2 F-9, 18 F-10.

West Helena, Arkansas
1 PT-13, 2 PT-17, 22 PT-19, 1 PT-22,
27 BT-15, 1 AT-17, 13 AT-10, 3 TG-3.

Wickenburg, Arizona
4 PT-17, 2 PT-22, 1 PT-27, 108 BT-13,
222 BT-15, 33 C-78, 3 A-24, 1 A-25.

Appendix 4

WAA SALES AND SALVAGE AIRCRAFT BY TYPE
JANUARY 24, 1946

The following planes were available for sale by the War Assets Administration at various fields throughout the United States in January 1946. Because of sales and additions these totals changed constantly, and the official term for this list is "For the week of January 24, 1946".

Part 1. ARMY AIR FORCES

Aircraft	Count
Northrop A-17	29
Vultee A-19	1
Douglas A-20	96
Douglas A-24	402
Curtiss A-25	106
Douglas A-26	28
Lockheed A-28	7
Lockheed A-29	30
Douglas A-33	4
Vultee A-35	5
North American A-36	36
North American AT-6	890
Beech AT-7	1
Cessna AT-8	1
Curtiss AT-9	462
Beech AT-10	1930
Beech AT-11	156
Republic AT-12	1
Noorduyn AT-16	1
Cessna AT-17	787
Lockheed AT-18	205
Fairchild AT-21	153
North American AT-24	1
Douglas B-7	1
Boeing B-17	3895
Douglas B-18	79
Douglas B-23	1
Consolidated B-24	5531
North American B-25	1084
Martin B-26	669
Consolidated B-32	104
Lockheed-Vega B-34	87
Boeing B-40	9
North American BC-1A	55
North American BT-9	10
Fleetwings BT-12	1
Vultee BT-13	4280
North American BT-14	7
Vultee BT-15	877
Douglas C-32	1
Douglas C-38	1
Curtiss C-46	475
Douglas C-47	417
Douglas C-49	4
Douglas C-53	9
Douglas C-54	117
Lockheed C-59	1
Lockheed C-60	49
Noorduyn C-64	26
Curtiss C-76	1
Cessna C-78	1735
Consolidated C-87	40
Consolidated C-109	2
Beech F-2	1
Douglas F-3	112
Lockheed F-5	74
Consolidated F-7	8
Boeing F-9	3
North American F-10	19
Taylorcraft L-2	1
Aeronca L-3	3
Piper L-4	27
Stinson L-5	74
Douglas O-46	5
North American O-47	47
Curtiss O-52	38
Grumman OA-12	1
Curtiss P-36	1
Lockheed P-38	851
Bell P-39	399

Curtiss P-40	1368
Republic P-43	2
Republic P-47	872
North American P-51	197
Northrop P-61	3
Bell P-63	287
North American P-64	4
Douglas P-70	74
Lockheed P-322	7
Bell P-400	10
Stearman PT-13	29
Stearman PT-17	463
Fairchild PT-19	78
Ryan PT-22	7
Fairchild PT-23	881
Stearman PT-27	22
Culver PQ-14	1
Lockheed-Vega R-37	79
North American TB-25	1

Part 2. NAVY

Grumman F4F	2
Grumman F6F	1151
Goodyear FG-1	366
General Motors FM-2	1382
Vought F4U-1	413
Cessna JRC-1	5
Grumman J2F	4
Grumman J2F-5	6
Grumman J2F-6	10
Grumman J4F-2	1
Piper NE-1	1
NAF N3N-3	77
Stearman N2S-1	17
Stearman N2S-2	14
Stearman N2S-4	357
Timm N2T-1	136
NAF OS2N-1	55
Vought OS2U	14
Vought OS2U-2	30
Vought OS2U-3	136
Boeing/Canada PB2B	5
North American PBJ-1	327
Martin PBM	100
Consolidated PBY-5	7
Consolidated PBY-5A	6
Consolidated PB4Y	354
Lockheed-Vega PV-1	268
Lockheed-Vega PV-3	10
Brewster SB2A	3
Curtiss SB2C	3
Douglas SBD-3	3
Douglas SBD-4	8
Douglas SBD-5	615
Douglas SBD-6	79
Fairchild-Canada SBF-1	72
CCF SBW-1	1
CCF SBW-3	70
Vultee SNV-1	956
Vultee SNV-2	342
Curtiss SO3C-1	3
Grumman TBF-1	376
General Motors TBM-1	582
General Motors TBM-3	2

Part 3. GLIDERS

Commonwealth CG-3	21
Frankfort TG-1	7
Schweizer TG-2	2
Schweizer TG-3	65
Aeronca TG-5	107
Taylorcraft TG-6	88
Aero Industries TG-31	1
Pratt-Read TG-32	50

Comments: The P-322 (Lockheed Model 322) was the "Lightning I" of the Royal Air Force but most of the contract was retained by the AAF. Likewise the P-400 was the designation for P-39s intended for the British. Both types were operated by the AAF using their RAF serial numbers. In a similar manner R-37 was the designation for the Lockheed-Vega "Ventura II" of the RAF and this was confusing because it was very similar to the AAF Model B-34. AJ368, photographed at Vail Field in Los Angeles in May 1946 had the designation "R Model 37" painted under the cockpit. A "J-5" is listed and is presumed to be a CAA Piper J-5A. The designation "B-30" is listed but there was no AAF B-30 built, so it is uncertain what these 13 aircraft were, but it is most likely that they were Lockheed-Vega B-34s. There is a listing for one "A-23" but there is no record of the experimental Martin XA-23 being sold surplus. This is probably a typographical error for the Douglas B-23.

Appendix 5

WAA Sales and Salvage Total by Class
January 31, 1946

Type of Aircraft	Salable	Salvage/Scrap
Liaison	333	
Utility Cargo	207	
Primary Trainers	2,573	
Basic Trainers	7,708	
Advanced Trainers	5,016	
Light Transport	1,948	
Medium Transport	751	
Heavy Transport	909	
Observation		351
Reconnaissance		335
Fighters		5,995
Light Bombers		2,428
Medium Bombers		2,749
Heavy Bombers		10,310
Patrol Bombers		207
Totals	19,4445	22,375
Grand Total	41,820	

Appendix 6

PRICE LIST FOR TACTICAL AIRCRAFT – 1946

Fixed prices were placed on Tactical type aircraft on January 24, 1946 by the War Assets Administration. Ranging from $32,500 for a Consolidated B-32 "superbomber", down to $350 for a Douglas O-46 observation plane, the prices were based largely on the type of plane and degree of obsolescence. While very few of these were eligible for certification by the Civil Aeronautics Administration for use in civil flying, the WAA had received a number of inquiries as to the possibility of purchasing these planes for varied purposes such as for ground study in commercial training schools, experimental flight, and for use by foreign governments.

Purchasers of tactical aircraft were required to accept full responsibility for applying for and obtaining the necessary operation permits from the CAA if the planes were to be used for flight purposes. The new prices did not apply to non-profit or tax-supported educational and other institutions that were allowed to purchase these planes at prices from $100 to $350 plus freight charges.

Aircraft Model	Price
A-17	$1,500
A-19	$500
A-20	$3,000
A-24 (SBD)	$1,650
A-25 (SB2C)	$3,000
A-26	$2,000
A-28 & A-29	$6,000
A-31 (V-72)	$1,000
A-33	$700
AT-12	$825
AT-21	$900
B-17	$13,750
B-18	$3,000
B-24	$13,750
B-25	$8,250
B-26	$3,000
B-29	$32,500
B-32	$32,500
B-34	$1,850
B-37 (O-56)	$1,950
B-40	$3,500
B-7	$1,150
F4F	$1,700
F4U-1	$1,250
F6F-3	$3,500
FG-1	$1,250
FM-2	$1,250
J2F-3, 4, 5, 6	$2,500
J3F (JRF)	$2,500
O-46	$350
O-47	$2,150
O-52	$1,225
OA-12	$3,450
OS2U	$1,350
OS2U-3	$1,350
P-36	$650
P-38	$1,250
P-39	$700
P-40	$1,250
P-400	$1,250
P-43	$1,250
P-47	$3,500
P-51	$3,500
P-61	$6,000
P-63	$1,000
P-64	$825
PB2B	$9,500
PB4Y	$13,750
PBM	$26,000
SB2A	$1,050
SNC-1	$500
SO3C-1	$1,250
TBF-1	$1,250
TBM-1	$1,250

Appendix 7

PRICE LIST FOR NON-TACTICAL AIRCRAFT
January 24, 1946

Aircraft Model	Price
AT-6	$850
AT-9	$1,500
AT-10	$7,500
AT-11	$7,500 to $15,000
AT-12	$825
AT-18	$6,000
AT-19	$1,500 to $2,500
AT-21	$900
BT-13	$975
BT-15	$975
C-70	$5,000
C-78/AT-17	$1,000 to $8,500
L-4	$750
L-5	$1,250
L-6	$750
PT-17/N2S	$875 to $2,400
PT-19	$875 to $2,400
PT-22	$875 to $2,400
PT-23	$875 to $2,400
PT-26	$875 to $2,400
AE-1	$1,000
GB-2	$5,000
NE-1	$1,490
N2T-1	$590 to $2,400
SNC-1	$500

Later reductions in prices reduced the cost for an AT-6 to $500, BT-13 to $450, C-70/GH to $2,000, PT-17/N2S to $250 and NE-1 $750.

Appendix 8

TRANSPORT AIRCRAFT PRICES
January 1946

The price for a useable transport was much higher than the price for a trainer or combat aircraft. The DC-3 type, being the most useful and saleable, had a specific breakdown in price according to condition that was not done with other surplus aircraft.

Beechcraft
    UC-45 $25,000 to $30,000
    AT-7 $20,000 to $25,000

Curtiss
    C-76 $16,000
    C-46 $25,000 to $40,000

Douglas
    C-32, C-33, C-34 $25,000
    C-38, C-39, C-42 $30,000
    C-47 - Run-of-the-Mill Cargo $20,000
    C-47 - Run-of-the-Mill Passenger $25,000
    C-47 - Recently overhauled Cargo $27,500
    C-47 - Recently overhauled Passenger $35,000
    C-47 - New Cargo $35,999
    C-47 - New Passenger $43,500

    DC-3 - Douglas Type (C-53, C-49, C-48 etc.
    DC-3 - Below average condition $30,000
    DC-3 - Average condition $40,000
    DC-3 - Above average condition $50,000

    C-54 - Series C-54 and C-54A $75,000
    C-54 - Series C-54B and C-54D $90,000
    C-54 - Series E and Subsequent Models $100,000

    C-67 $20,000 to $25,000

Lockheed
    C-36A (Model 10) $27,500
    C-40A (Model 12A) $23,800
    C-56, C-57, C-59, C-60, C-66, R5O (Model 18) $20,000 to $35,000

Noorduyn
    UC-64 $7,000 to $10,000

Appendix 9

CIVIL AIRCRAFT SALES

One of the lesser known activities of the War Assets Administration was the sale of "Surplus Government Property - Aircraft" that were not military and never had a military serial number. These were government owned aircraft operated in the Civilian Pilot Training Program (CPTP) in World War II as well as a variety of types flown by the Civil Aeronautics Administration (CAA).

A partial list of these offered for sale through the Atlanta Regional Office of WAA in April 1946 is a good example of these sales offerings.

EAGLE FIELD, DOS PALOS, CALIFORNIA

Ryan STA NC-9; Beech E-17B NC-91; Beech D-17S WTS-60, Stinson Reliant SR-9E NC-84; Fairchild 24K NC-266; CW Travel Air B-14B NC-1A; Howard DGA-15P NC-65; Howard DGA-8 NC-57; Piper J3C-65 NC-195, NC-38947; Piper J4A NC-105, NC-107, NC-116; Fairchild M62A NC-146, NC-204, NC-205, NC-207; Waco ZKS-7 NC-49; Waco UPF-7 NC-166, NC-167, NC-168, NC-169, NC-219, NC-220.

CIMARRON FIELD, YUKON, OKLAHOMA

Waco EGC NC-8; Waco AGC NC-61; Fairchild M62A NC-135, NC-137, NC-139, NC-206, NC-301; Beech E-17B NC-114; Piper J4A NC-124; Fairchild 24G NC-45; Piper J-3C NC-41173, NC-41457; Howard DGA-8 NC-58; Stinson SR-9C NC-76; Stinson SR-8B NC-74, NC-75; Waco AGC-8 NC-60; Fairchild 24W-41A NC-57924; Ercoupe 415-C NC-144.

WOODWARD FIELD, CAMDEN, SOUTH CAROLINA

Stinson HW-75 NC-72, NC-112; Stinson SR-9E NC-83; Fairchild 24W-9 NC-97, NC-98; Cessna C-165 NC-125; Piper J4A NC-106, NC-123; Waco UPF-7 NC-152, NC-154, NC-155, NC-173; Howard DGA-8 NC-55, NC-56; Waco AGC-8 NC-62; Stinson SR-9E NC-87; Stinson SR-8B NC-81; Harlow PJC-2 NC-102; Stinson SR-8C NC-77; Fairchild 24-W9 NC-101; Fairchild 24G NC-19, NC-51, NC-187; Fairchild M62A NC-134, NC-150, NC-208, NC-210, NC-211; Interstate S1B1 NC-73.

There are some interesting footnotes to this listing:
1. Five L-5's located at Camden, NC are earmarked for the Department of Interior. Nineteen L-4's at Camden, SC are earmarked for Government Agencies and for Veterans.
2. The one J-5 located at Jackson, TN is not available for sale.
3. PT-17 Boeing Stearman aircraft at Decatur, AL; Dos Palos, CA; and El Reno, OK are stored inside hangars, all have wings removed, and are prepared for long term storage; they will be assembled when sold.
4. PT-23 Fairchild aircraft at Cape Girardeau, MO, and Union City, TN are eligible for temporary certification by CAA, pending installation of Lord Anti-Vibration engine mounts. These are available from Fairchild for $55.65 FOB Hagerstown, MD.
5. N2T-1 Navy Timm aircraft at Cape Girardeau, MO are eligible for CAA certification on the merits of each aircraft. WAC and CAA Inspectors have inspected each aircraft and a copy of the inspection report is with each aircraft.
6. The Civil Aeronautics Administration is now in the process of transferring flyable surplus aircraft to their needs to Camden, SC, Oklahoma City, OK, and Dos Palos, CA. Under the new policy, single

engine aircraft under 5000 pounds gross weight are to be Price Tagged in order to give Veterans Preference. Any grounded CAA aircraft will be sold whenever possible on the bid basis "where is, as is."

These "Personal Aircraft" were sold on a priority basis. Prior to January 29, 1946, all personal type aircraft (such as Liaison, single-engine Utility Cargo under 6,000 pounds gross weight, Grumman Widgeons, Beechcraft, Waco, and Fairchilds) that were in flyable condition were sold on the Invitation to Bids system. The prices varied from $1,150 (Piper J3C) to $7,225 (Waco AGC). Two planes that must have been in excellent condition had a much higher price: Beech D-17S at $17,250 and a Howard DGA-15P at $17,900.

In May 1946 this was changed to a priority system; First Priority was to Federal Government Agencies. Second Priority was to State and Local Governments. Third Priority was to Veterans of World War II. The final category was the general public, called non-priority groups.

Appendix No. 10

AAF IMPRESSED CIVIL AIRCRAFT DECLARED SURPLUS

When the United States entered World War II in 1941 there was a need for the military to obtain as many useable civilian aircraft as possible. Most of these were four-place cabin planes to be used for staff transport. Aircraft owners were asked to donate or sell their planes to the Government and as a result hundreds of small civilian planes were impressed into duty with the Army and Navy. (See Chapter 2 for a discussion of similar Navy aircraft). Beginning in late 1944 when new production had replaced their need the majority were declared surplus and turned over to the Reconstruction Finance Corporation for sale. The following table lists all of these aircraft used by the AAF with their former NC Numbers and the date declared surplus.

AAF Serial No	AAF Model	Registration	Date	Aircraft Type
42-36825	UC-43C	NC2595	08-19-45	Beech F17D
42-38217	OA-14	NC26679	08-05-45	Grumman G-44
42-38219	OA-14	NC1230	04-01-45	Grumman G-44
42-38221	OA-14	NC37182	08-17-45	Grumman G-44
42-38223	OA-14	NC28667	07-10-45	Grumman G-44
42-38229	UC-43A	NC20752	10-12-44	Beech D17R
42-38230	UC-43A	NC21919	02-14-45	Beech D17R
42-38235	UC-43B	NC18582	02-14-45	Beech D17S
42-38239	UC-43C	NC20789	11-05-44	Beech F17D
42-38240	UC-43C	NC20786	02-21-45	Beech F17D
42-38241	UC-43C	NC20772	11-23-44	Beech F17D
42-38246	UC-43C	NC19454	12-06-44	Beech F17D
42-38247	UC-43C	NC303W	11-15-44	Beech F17D
42-38261	C-56A	NC17395	-	Lockheed 18
42-38266	UC-71	NC17657	01-31-45	Spartan 7W
42-38267	UC-71	NC17631	12-20-44	Spartan 7W
42-38271	UC-72	NC20961	11-23-44	Waco SRE
42-38272	UC-72	NC20969	03-08-45	Waco SRE
42-38283	UC-43C	NC19451	08-22-45	Beech F17D
42-38284	UC-43C	NC289Y	10-17-44	Beech F17D
42-38288	UC-71	NC17656	01-23-45	Spartan 7W
42-38298	UC-81E	NC18441	12-30-44	Stinson SR-9F
42-38301	UC-81F	NC18479	03-11-45	Stinson SR-10F
42-38339	OA-14	NC37183	04-20-45	Grumman G-44
42-38340	OA-14	NC777	03-08-45	Grumman G-44
42-38361	UC-43C	NC238Y	12-06-44	Beech F17D
42-38364	UC-70	NC22412	10-06-44	Howard DGA-15P
42-38365	UC-70	NC22410	02-26-45	Howard DGA-15P
42-38366	UC-70	NC22429	10-03-44	Howard DGA-15P
42-38367	UC-71	NC17633	01-31-45	Spartan 7W

Appendices

42-38368	UC-71	NC17615	09-28-44	Spartan 7W
42-38369	UC-71	NC17664	09-18-44	Spartan 7W
42-38371	UC-72	NC31657	03-08-45	Waco SRE
42-38374	UC-72A	NC4400	02-23-45	Cessna T-50
42-38375	UC-78A	NC21939	10-4-44	Cessna T-50
42-38379	UC-78A	NC27299	09-26-44	Cessna T-50
42-43517	UC-43C	NC20754	01-12-45	Beech F17D
42-43618	UC-70	NC22407	10-30-44	Howard DGA
42-43621	C-49E	NC21769	01-29-45	Douglas DST
42-43846	UC-71	NC20200	11-10-44	Spartan 7W
42-46906	UC-43C	NC18762	02-23-44	Beech F17D
42-46908	UC-43C	NC18568	02-14-45	Beech F17D
42-46909	UC-43D	NC18042	10-26-44	Beech E17B
42-46915	UC-43D	NC18587	02-14-45	Beech E17B
42-46916	UC-43C	NC248Y	05-15-45	Beech F17D
42-47386	UC-43C	NC3048	09-19-44	Beech F17D
42-47442	UC-43D	NC17071	11-6-44	Beech E17B
42-47443	UC-43D	NC18044	03-05-45	Beech E17B
42-47444	UC-43D	NC17091	10-17-44	Beech E17B
42-47445	UC-43D	NC18560	03-05-45	Beech E17B
42-47446	UC-43D	NC18585	11-11-44	Beech E17B
42-47447	UC-43D	NC17083	02-14-45	Beech E17B
42-47449	UC-43C	NC20771	-	Beech F17D
42-47450	UC-43C	NC18573	11-15-44	Beech F17D
42-47451	UC-70D	NC22434	02-16-45	Howard DGA
42-49070	UC-43D	NC18041	10-9-44	Beech E17B
42-49071	UC-43F	NC18453	02-22-45	Beech D17A
42-49073	UC-81H	NC80Y	02-14-45	Stinson SR-10E
42-49075	UC-70B	NC1227	06-22-45	Howard DGA-15J
42-49076	UC-70B	NC22418	09-14-44	Howard DGA-15J
42-52999	UC-43A	NC15817	09-04-44	Beech D17R
42-53000	UC-43D	NC18787	09-28-44	Beech E17B
42-53004	UC-70	NC22406	01-30-45	Howard DGA-15P
42-53005	UC-43D	NC18785	01-04-44	Beech E17B
42-53006	UC-43G	NC17092	10-6-44	Beech C17B
42-53007	UC-43D	NC18588	02-14-45	Beech E17B
42-53009	UC-81F	NC2429	11-24-44	Stinson SR-10F
42-53509	UC-43D	NC18784	02-14-45	Beech E17B
42-53510	UC-45C	NC20756	02-05-46	Beech 18S
42-53511	UC-43D	NC19467	10-27-44	Beech E17B
42-53513	UC-80	NC19996	01-24-45	Harlow PJC-2
42-53517	UC-43D	NC903	02-21-45	Beech E17B
42-53524	UC-81	NC17125	08-04-45	Stinson SR-8B
42-56086	UC-81A	NC23722	11-23-44	Stinson SR-10G
42-56087	UC-43D	NC17085	11-5-44	Beech E17B
42-56088	UC-81J	NC18437	10-7-44	Stinson SR-9F
42-56091	C-48B	NC18107	04-23-45	Douglas DST
42-56092	C-49E	NC16005	02-08-45	Douglas DST

42-56639	UC-36A	NC1061	01-19-45	Lockheed 10A
42-57156	C-32A	NC13790	05-22-45	Douglas DC-2
42-57224	C-56D	NC36604	12-27-44	Lockheed 18-08
42-57225	UC-81A	NC27792	10-12-44	Stinson SR-10G
42-57510	UC-81B	NC17102	06-27-45	Stinson SR-8D
42-57512	C-84	NC17319	03-15-45	Douglas DC-3B
42-61093	UC-43D	NC18775	02-14-45	Beech E17B
42-61095	C-32A	NC13716	05-15-45	Douglas DC-2
42-61098	UC-81C	NC18410	06-11-45	Stinson SR-10C
42-62607	UC-81J	NC17137	12-20-44	Stinson SR-9E
43-62608	UC-81J	NC18444	11-23-44	Stinson SR-9E
42-66385	UC-86	NC28502	04-24-45	Fairchild 24R40
42-68339	UC-43A	NC17082	10-06-45	Beech D17R
42-68341	UC-72C	NC1252	12-28-44	Waco HRE
42-68342	UC-72C	NC31654	10-17-44	Waco HRE
42-68344	UC-81K	NC18480	01-24-45	Stinson SR-10C
42-68346	UC-81K	NC22555	06-10-44	Stinson SR-10C
42-68361	UC-71	NC17605	10-30-44	Spartan 7W
42-68368	C-73	NC13329	06-06-45	Boeing 247D
42-68675	UC-88	NC16877	02-14-45	Fairchild 45
42-68678	UC-72B	NC-2279	01-8-44	Waco EGC
42-68685	UC-81J	NC17188	03-30-45	Stinson SR-9E
42-68691	UC-81C	NC21108	10-12-44	Stinson SR-9C
42-68852	UC-86	NC28530	11-23-44	Fairchild 24R40
42-68857	C-32A	NC13787	03-22-44	Douglas DC-2
42-68858	C-32A	NC13720	04-26-45	Douglas DC-2
42-70862	UC-61C	NC18653	10-31-44	Fairchild 24A9
42-78016	UC-72D	NC2307	10-17-44	Waco VKS-7
42-78020	UC-81G	NC17186	02-23-44	Stinson SR-9D
42-78022	UC-94	NC21946	05-31-45	Cessna 165
42-78023	UC-77D	NC18596	08-09-45	Cessna C37
42-78024	UC-77D	NC18047	01-23-44	Cessna C37
42-78029	UC-86	NC25325	04-06-45	Fairchild 24H
42-78035	UC-72E	NC2218	10-26-44	Waco ZGC-7
42-78037	UC-71	NC17661	05-11-45	Spartan 7W
42-78040	UC-86	NC25331	10-24-44	Fairchild 24H
42-78042	UC-81G	NC17109	11-23-43	Stinson SR-9D
42-79548	UC-92	RX2	-	Funk B75L
42-79549	UC-90A	RX24	-	Luscombe 8B
42-79550	UC-90	RX25	-	Luscombe 8A
42-88613	UC-61F	NC18686	01-28-46	Fairchild 34R9
42-88616	UC-70	NC22426	09-19-44	Howard DGA
42-88629	UC-43G	NC16443	09-29-44	Beech C17B
42-88634	UC-43G	NC15845	10-18-44	Beech C17B
42-88636	UC-43C	NC2626	10-21-44	Beech F17D
42-88637	UC-81E	NC20605	10-08-44	Fairchild 24K
42-94126	UC-72K	NC17713	02-19-45	Waco YKS7
42-94127	UC-81G	NC296Y	11-23-44	Fairchild 24W

Appendices

42-94129	UC-72H	NC16220	02-14-45	Waco ZQC6
42-94131	UC-72H	NC15709	10-19-44	Waco ZQC6
42-94134	UC-81M?	NC3640	19-12-44	Stinson SR-9E
42-94135	UC-72M?	NC20954	11-23-44	Waco ZKS7
42-94139	UC-61E	NC8495	01-30-46	Fairchild 24K
42-94141	UC-72K	NC19353	02-26-45	Waco VKS7
42-94142	UC-86	NC25392	11-22-44	Fairchild 24R
42-94147	UC-61	NC41844	09-18-44	Fairchild 24W
42-94148	UC-101	NC14236	09-01-44	Lockheed 5C
42-97033	UC-78A	NC34754	01-29-45	Cessna T-50
42-97035	UC-78A	NC34758	03-01-45	Cessna T-50
42-97037	UC-78A	NC34760	02-28-45	Cessna T-50
42-97038	UC-78A	NC34761	01-14-45	Cessna T-50
42-97040	UC-80	NC19997	12-23-44	Harlow PJC2
42-97044	C-103	NC1051	-	Grumman G-32A
42-97045	C-103	NC1326	01-27-45	Grumman G-32A
42-97046	C-102	NC41667	11-23-44	Rearwin 9000
42-97047	C-102	NC20733	09-11-44	Rearwin 9000
42-97049	UC-43C	NC291Y	12-23-44	Beech F17D
42-97050	UC-43C	NC2801	11-06-44	Beech F17D
42-97051	L-9B	NC39456	11-23-44	Stinson 10A
42-97052	UC-72H	NC16586	02-14-45	Waco ZQC6
42-97054	UC-80	NC18798	11-23-44	Harlow PJC2
42-97056	UC-81K	NC1920	09-01-44	Stinson SR-10C
42-97057	UC-81J	NC18454	12-23-44	Stinson SR-9E
42-97414	UC-61H	NC18116	09-05-44	Fairchild 24G
42-97415	UC-43G	NC17079	09-04-44	Beech C17B
42-97420	UC-43J	NC15836	02-14-45	Beech C17L
42-97421	UC-72Q	NC16206	02-14-45	Waco ZQC
42-97424	UC-43E	NC1600	10-17-44	Beech C17R
42-97425	UC-72J	NC18370	02-14-45	Waco AVN8
42-97426	UC-43G	NC16439	10-19-44	Beech C17B
42-97429	UC-72M	NC2628	11-23-44	Waco ZKS7
42-97430	L-9B	NC32271	08-28-44	Stinson 10A
42-97432	L-9B	NC31538	11-27-44	Stinson 10A
42-97433	UC-61G	NC28645	09-15-44	Fairchild 24W
42-97435	UC-61A	NC37194	01-23-44	Fairchild 24W
42-107276	UC-61J	NC16815	11-23-44	Fairchild 24C8F
42-107277	UC-43K	NC18562	11-27-44	Beech D17W
42-107278	L-9B	NC31548	09-17-44	Stinson 10A
42-107279	UC-70B	NC22421	05-22-45	Howard DGA-15J
42-107400	C-94	NC32548	09-04-44	Cessna 165
42-107406	L-9B	NC31596	09-19-44	Stinson 10A
42-107407	L-9B	NC32858	10-17-44	Stinson 10A
42-107408	L-9B	NC31514	09-28-44	Stinson 10A
42-107409	L-9B	NC34602	09-01-44	Stinson 10A
42-107410	L-9B	NC31589	08-24-44	Stinson 10A
42-107411	UC-43C	NC20797	02-07-44	Beech E17D

42-107412	L-10	NC18916	11-23-44	Ryan SCW
42-107413	C-102A	NC27719	01-09-44	Rearwin 8135
42-107414	UC-43C	NC19473	01-05-45	Beech F17D
42-107416	UC-81	NC16191	10-17-44	Stinson SR-8B
42-107325	L-4F	NC38292	04-22-45	Piper J5A
44-52988	L-4F	NC40658	04-22-45	Piper J5A
44-52989	UC-81	NC15111	-	Stinson SR-8B
44-52993	UC-81J	-	10-34-44	Stinson SR-9F
44-52994	L-12	-	02-14-45	Stinson SR-5A
44-52995	L-12A	-	02-12-45	Stinson SM-7B

Excerpt from Whittle, "Civil Aircraft Impressed Into USAAF During World War II."

Appendix 11

VULTEE BT AIRCRAFT FOR SALE

One of the major sales items in the immediate post war period was the Vultee BT-13/15 and Navy SNV-1/2 sales. The low price of the BT-13s led to their purchase by many crop dusters solely for the use of the Pratt & Whitney 450 hp engines. The successful modification of their use on the Stearman PT-17 by Lloyd Stearman for Inland Aviation at Los Banos, California, in April 1946 led to the widespread introduction of the 450 hp Wasp Stearman duster and sprayer.

The BT's could be purchased as fly-away planes or as scrap to be trucked away from the sales depots. The total available at the following WAA Sales-Storage Depots was 5,237. Of these 1,918 were in Texas and 960 in Oklahoma. The highest number of civil registered BT-13/15's appears to be 4,057 in January 1949.

Location	Number
Albuquerque, NM	21
Americus, GA	1
Augusta, GA	234
Ballinger, TX	288
Blythe, CA	279
Camden, SC	159
Clinton, OK	384
Cuero, TX	40
Decatur, IL	288
Dos Palos, CA	133
Fort Stockton, TX	354
Fort Worth, TX	219
Jackson, TN	243
Kingman, AZ	1
Lamesa, TX	293
Madison, MS	18
Muskogee, OK	9
Oklahoma City, OK	490
Ontario, CA	28
Phoenix, AZ	14
Pine Bluff, AR	120
Ponca City, OK	77
Stamford, TX	52
Tucson, AZ	10
Union City, TN	350
Vernon, TX	672
Walnut Ridge, AR	187
Wickenburg, AZ	273

Appendix 12

FAA AIRCRAFT CODES

When the FAA established a computer system in the 1950's Aircraft Codes were assigned to all registered aircraft. The first published list of these was in 1963 with the establishment of the printed civil registers sold by the Government Printing Office. This excerpt from the June 1, 1963 Register is evidence that at least one of each of these World War II surplus types existed.

Code	Aircraft	Code	Aircraft
115-01	Beech AT-10	526-01	Lockheed B-34
115-02	Beech AT-11	526-02	Lockheed P-38
118-01	Bell P-39	545-01	Martin B-26
118-02	Bell P-63	545-02	Martin PBM-5
138-02	Boeing B-17	612-01	Naval Aircraft Factory N3N-1
138-16	Boeing YC-97	612-02	Naval Aircraft Factory N3N-3
161-05	Budd RB-1	633-01	Noorduyn AT-16
193-01	Canadian-Vickers Stranraer	633-02	Noorduyn UC-64
242-02	Convair BT-13	640-01	North American A-36A
242-03	Convair BT-15	640-04	North American AT-6
242-08	Convair LB-30	640-07	North American B-25
242-10	Convair PB2Y	640-09	North American BC-1
242-11	Convair P4Y-2	640-10	North American BC-1A
242-12	Convair PBY-5	640-12	North American BT-9
242-13	Convair PBY-6	640-13	North American BT-14
262-01	Curtiss AT-9	640-22	North American O-47B
262-20	Curtiss O-52	640-23	North American P-51
262-21	Curtiss P-36	645-04	Northrop P-61
262-22	Curtiss P-40	710-02	Piper AE-1/HE-1
262-23	Curtiss SB2C	710-09	Piper L-14
262-26	Curtiss C-46 Cargo	757-01	Republic AT-12
262-27	Curtiss C-46 Passenger	757-04	Republic P-47
362-03	Douglas A-20	765-01	Avro Anson V
362-04	Douglas A-24	783-01	Ryan PT-20
362-05	Douglas A-26	792-03	St. Louis YPT-15
362-06	Douglas B-18	814-01	Sikorsky R-4B
362-07	Douglas B-23	814-02	Sikorsky R-5A
362-09	Douglas C-74	863-01	Stinson L-1
313-01	Seversky P-35 (Doyle)	863-02	Stinson L-5
337-10	Fairchild AT-21	873-04	Culver PQ-14 (Superior)
343-05	Federal XPT-1	885-01	Taylorcraft Army TG-6
387-05	Goodyear FG-1	898-02	Timm N2T-1
395-01	Grumman FM-2	910-01	DeHavilland Mosquito (Transworld)
395-08	Grumman F8F		
395-02	Grumman J2F		
395-03	Grumman TBF/TBM		
395-06	Grumman F6F		

Appendix 13

CAA Aircraft Totals For 1947

Some indication of how many surplus aircraft were registered (assigned an N Number) by the Civil Aeronautics Administration is documented by the following excerpt from the November 1, 1947 "Statistical Study of Registered Civil Aircraft."

An interesting comment about the effect of World War II on record keeping, as well as everything else involved in aviation, is contained in this portion of the introduction to this document:

"Contained herein are the results of a statistical study made by the Aviation Statistics Division of the Civil Aeronautics Administration of the 92,644 registered aircraft in the United States on record with the Administration on November 1, 1947. This is the figure available at the present time, and is substantially correct. The war years, however, exacted their toll of the aircraft records of the Civil Aeronautics Administration, and many safeguards intended to protect the reliability of the records were the victims of more pressing demands."

Government record keepers and statisticians are very careful to list exactly what the document says. Thus the odd designation "P63A6" used by the CAA really refers to the AAF Block Number "P-63A-6-BE". If these were not methodically copied down, and an IBM Code for each assigned, the total for P-63A's registered in 1947 would be three aircraft.

Aeronca L-3B	2	Convair BT-13	114
Aeronca O-58A	9	Convair BT-12A	2,264
Aeronca O-58B	811	Convair BT-13B	590
		Convair BT-15	193
Beech AT-10	1	Convair SNV-1	182
Beech AT-11	72	Convair SNV-2	114
Beech AT-11B	1	Convair PB2Y-5Z	1
		Convair (Vultee) A-31C	1
Bell P-39	2	Convair XA-41	1
Bell P-39L	1		
Bell P-63	2	Curtiss C-46A	3
Bell P-63A	1	Curtiss C-46E	10
Bell P-63A6	1	Curtiss O-52	3
Bell P-63A7	1	Curtiss P-36A	1
Bell P-63C5	1	Curtiss YP-60E	1
Bell P-63E	2	Curtiss SNC-1	3
Bell P-63E1	2	Curtiss SO3C-1	1
		Curtiss SO3C-2	1
Boeing B-17F	1		
		Douglas A-20G	2
Canadian-Vickers Stranraer	4	Douglas RA-24B	1
		Douglas A-26	6

Douglas A-26B	2
Douglas A-26C	4
Douglas B-18	14
Douglas B-18A	9
Douglas B-18B	2
Douglas B-23	4
Douglas C-54	1
Douglas C-54A	68
Douglas C-54B	176
Douglas C-54DC	23
Douglas C-54E	20
Douglas C-54G	15
Douglas UC-67 (B-23)	16
Douglas R5D-1	1
Fairchild AT-21	4
Fairchild PT-19A	1
Goodyear FG-1	1
Goodyear FG-1D	1
Grumman FM-2	1
Grumman TBF-1	1
Grumman TBM-1C	1
Kellett YO-60	1
Lockheed AT-18	3
Lockheed AT-18A	1
Lockheed RA-28	1
Lockheed C-69	1
Lockheed XC-69E	1
Lockheed F-5G	11
Lockheed P-38	2
Lockheed P-38L	16
Lockheed P-38M	6
Naval Aircraft Factory N3N-1	1
Naval Aircraft Factory N3N-3	446
Noorduyn UC-64	4
Noorduyn UC-64A	105
Noorduyn UC-64B	3
North American A-36A	1
North American AT-6	3
North American AT-6A	367
North American AT-6B	104
North American AT-6C	62
North American BC-1A	1
North American SNJ-2	20
North American SNJ-3	82
North American SNJ-4	132
North American P-51A	1
North American P-51B	1
North American P-51C	2
North American P-51D	8
Piper L-14	3
Republic AT-12	2
Ryan PT-21	1
Stearman N2S-3	1
Stearman N2S-4	1
Stinson L-1	1
Stinson L-5	111
Stinson L-5E1	1
Stinson L-5G	24
Timm N2T-1	100
Vought SB2U-1	1

Appendix 14

ADDITIONAL CAA AIRCRAFT TOTALS FOR 1949

An interesting phenomenon occurs in the Statistical Study for July 1, 1949. The following is a list of World War II aircraft types that are listed for 1949 but are not in the 1947 report. This raises the question as to whether these planes were registered in 1947 but not found in the CAA records or if there was a refinement in classification.

The registration system is based entirely upon the forms submitted by the aircraft owner. This is very apparent in the differences in lists of the same kind of plane. The most obvious is the Stearman Model 75. Most of these are reported by the owner as the model shown on the factory nameplate, such as Model "A75N1", which explains their high totals. But some owners will use the AAF nameplate and list it as an AAF PT-17 or a Navy N2S-4 etc. The same confusion occurs with the serial number of the plane; it could be the factory serial, the AAF serial or a Navy serial and all are correct. A North American AT-6D, for example, could be 88-17242 (NAA) or 42-85461 (AAF). An SNJ-4 can be 88-14124 (NAA) or 51542 (USN). Whatever is on the original Bill of Sale will remain with the FAA records and, as many warbird owners have discovered, is extremely difficult to change.

The ex RCAF PT-26s could have been included in the totals for the Fairchild M-62A in 1947, and the Cessna UC-78s were probably a part of the 1,420 T-50s listed. A real question remains, however, about the Grumman J2F Ducks. There are none in the 1947 report, even under their company designation G-15, and yet they were sold surplus in 1946. Therefore the following types should be added to those in Appendix 13.

Boeing B-17G	6	Goodyear FG-1	1
		Goodyear FG-1D	1
Budd RB-1	4	Goodyear F2G-1	1
		Goodyear F2G-2	2
Cessna AT-17	31	Goodyear XF2G	1
Cessna UC-78	62		
		Grumman J2F-3	1
Convair PB4Y-1	1	Grumman J2F-4	1
		Grumman J2F-5	1
Culver PQ-14A	2	Grumman J2F-6	6
Culver PQ-14B	2	Grumman JRF-6B	2
Culver TD2C-1	1		
		Howard NH-1	3
Curtiss O-52	3		
		Lockheed C-60A	6
Douglas A-20K	1	Lockheed P-38E	1
Douglas C-47	4	Lockheed PV-1	13
Douglas C-47B	1	Lockheed-Vega RB-37	1
Douglas RB-18	1		
Douglas RB-18B	1	Martin PBM-5	2
Douglas SBD-5	1		
		Noorduyn YC-64	1
Fairchild PT-19A	5		
Fairchild PT-23	26	North American B-25C	1
Fairchild PT-26	12	North American B-25D	3

North American B-25H	1
North American BC-1	1
North American BC-1A	9
North American BT-14	1
North American P-51C	6
North American P-51K	3
Piper L-4H	1
Piper L-4J	3
Republic P-47	1
Sikorsky R-4B	10
Stearman N2S-1	3
Stearman N2S-5	37
Stearman PT-13D	2
Stearman PT-17	36
Taylorcraft L-2A	1
Taylorcraft L-2B	2
United Aircraft (Vought) OS2U-2	1
Waco UC-72Q	1

BIBLIOGRAPHY

"Acres of Aircraft", Naval Aviation News, April 1948, pg. 20

Advance Release, War Assets Administration, Washington, DC. No. 868 December 16, 1946; No. 1011 February 1, 1947; No. 1021 February 4, 1947; No. 1022 February 4, 1947; No. 1079 February 17, 1947; No. 1112 March 3, 1947; 1241 April 24, 1947; No. 1344 June 8, 1947; No. 1369 June 27, 1947; No. 1399 July 22, 1947..

Aircraft and Components - 1946, Report No. 470-W-4, Progress Analysis Division, WAA.

Aircraft Listing July 1, 1949, Civil Aviation Administration, Office of Aviation Safety. (A condensed listing of specifications pertaining to older aircraft models of which not more than 50 individual aircraft are still in service).

Alphabetical Index of Aircraft Specifications, Office of Flight Operations and Airworthiness, U. S. Department of Commerce, Civil Aeronautics Administration, January 2, 1958.

Alphabetical Index of Technical Publications, AAF Technical Order No. 00-2. 15 May 1944.

Army Air Forces Installations Directory, Continental United States, 1 December, 1944, Hq AAF, Washington, DC.

Baker, Brian R., "Surplus Aircraft at Litchfield Park." American Aviation Historical Society Journal, Vol 1, No 3, April-June 1958, pp 131-132.

Birdsall, Steve, "Arizona Sundown: The Twilight of the Aluminum Goddesses," Air Classics, December 1969, pp 14-21.

Birdsall, Steve and Greer, Don, B-17 Flying Fortress in Color, Squadron/Signal Publications, 1986.

Blue, Allan G., The B-24 Liberator, Charles Scribner's Sons, NY.

Chapman, John, Coggan, Paul and Goodall, Geoff, Warbirds Directory Third Edition, Warbirds Worldwide, June 1996.

Chinnery, Philip, Desert Boneyard, Airlife (England) 1987

"Clippers For Sale, $50,000 each while they last as surplus," Flying, August 1946, pp 50-51.

Cupido, Joe, Chino: Warbird Treasures Past & Present, Fox-2 Productions, 2000.

Fahey, James C., U. S. Army Aircraft 1908-1946, Ships and Aircraft, 1946.

Farmer, James H., "Saga of the Civil Forts: Part 1 - The Era of the W.A.A. and the Years of Plenty," American Aviation Historical Society Journal, Vol 22, No 4, Winter 1977, pp 292-302.

Grossnick, Roy A., United States Naval Aviation 1910-1995, Naval Historical Center, Department of the Navy, Washington, DC, 1997.

History of AF Storage and Withdrawal Program 1945-52, U. S. Air Force, 129 pp.

How To Buy Surplus Aircraft, Parts, and Miscellaneous Air Equipment, Office of Aircraft Disposal, War Assets Administration, Washington, DC, 1946.

Juptner, Joseph P., U. S. Civil Aircraft, Aero Publishers, Fallbrook, CA. Nine Volumes published between 1962 and 1981. Covers ATC-1 to ATC-817.

Kroger, William, "Junking of Old Planes Pressed Before Economy Clamor Rises," Aviation News, November 26, 1945, pp 11-14.

"Larger Dealer Role in Disposal of Surplus PTs Appears Justified," Aviation News, March 12, 1945, pg 15.

Larkins, William T., "War Album," The Aeroplane Spotter (England), June 14, 1947, pg 128.

Larkins, William T. "U. S. Civil Registrations - The Story of Their Evolution," Air Pictorial (England), April 1954, pp 104-106.

Larkins, William T. "U. S. Civil Registrations- The Story of Their Evolution Part 2," Air Pictorial (England), May 1954, pp 141-143.

Larkins, William T., "Forgotten Warbird Graveyard." Air Classics Quarterly Review, Winter 1978, pp 44-57.

Larkins, William T., "Kingman, Arizona - 1947, A Personal View," Aerophile, Vol 2 No 1, June 1979, pp 16-25.

Larkins, William T., "War Assets," Part 1, Air Classics, February 1992, pp 17-28, 54-59; Part 2, Air Classics, March 1992, pp 12-25, 62-67; Part 3, Air Classics, April 1992, pp 16-29, 66-71.

Larkins, William T., "How We Destroyed Our World War Two Air Force." Military Surplus Warplanes, Vol 1, 1995, pp 4-42, 70-73. Re-arranged reprint of the three-part 1992 Air Classics series.

Larkins, William T., "Chino's Ghostly Warbirds." Warbirds International, May-June 2002, pp 44-5

Malayney, Norm, "Destroy The Warbirds!," Warbirds International, January/February 1993, pp 50-58.

McDowell, Ernest R., and Ward, Richard, Consolidated B-24D-M Liberator in USAAF-RAF-RAAF-MLD-IAF-CzechAF & CNAF Service PB4Y-1/2 Privateer in USN-USMC-Aeronavale & CNAF Service, Arco-Aircam Aviation Series No. 11, Vol 1, Osprey 1969.

McLain, Jerry, "Warbirds Swansong," Arizona Highways, May 1947, pp 1, 38, 39 plus cover.

McLain, Jerry, "Warbirds Swansong," Aero Album, Vol 8, Winter 1969, pp 3-7.

Miller, J. J. and Patterson, Guy, "Death of an Air Force," Flying, November 1947, pp 22-23

Bibliography

Miller, J. J., "The Aircraft Graveyard," Impact/Albuquerque Journal Magazine, October 19, 1982, pp 8-10.

Miscellaneous - Unit Costs of Aircraftr and Engines, AAF Technical Order No. 00-25-30, 8 January 1945, 108pp.

Model Designations Of Army Aircraft, Air Technical Service Command, AAF, January 1945.

Model Designation of Naval Aircraft, NAVAER 00-25Q-13, April 1945, Navy Department, Bureau of Aeronautics, Washington, DC.

Modern Electric Guillotine Speeds Salvage of Aluminum From Obsolete Navy Planes, NAS Norfolk Press Release, April 4, 1948, U. S. Navy.

Moll, Nigel, "Ghost Story," Flying, February 2989, pp 69-75.

Munday, E. A., Fifteenth Air Force Combat Markings 1943-1945, Beaumont Publication, London, no date.

Munday, E. A. and Ward, Richard, USAAF Heavy Bomb Group Markings & Camouflage 1941-1945 Boeing B-17 Flying Fortress, Aircam Aviation Series No. S14, Osprey Publishing (England) 1973.

Naval Aeronautic Publications Index, September 1944, NavAir 00-500, Office of CNO and Bureau of Aeronautics, U.S. Navy.

"Navy Guillotine Chops Up Planes for Salvage," Naval Aviation News, April 1948, pg 25.

O'Leary, Michael, "Mosquitos In American Skies," Military Surplus Warplanes, Vol. 1, 1995. Publishing, 1973.

O'Leary, Michael and Peltzer, Milo, "Return To Kingman," Air Classics, May 1997, pp 23-33 67-70.

Pearcy, Arthur, Lend-Lease Aircraft In World War II, Airlife (England), 1996.

Peltzer, Milo and O'Leary, Michael, "Ghosts of Litchfield Park," Military Surplus Warplanes, Fall 1997, pp 4-21.

"Planes Go Begging," Business Week, April 28, 1945, pg. 108.

Quarterly Progress Report By The Surplus Property Board To The Congress, 28 May 1945, 108 pp.

Record of Acceptances 1935-1946 (Naval Aircraft), Bureau of Aeronautics, Navy Department, Washington, DC.

RFC, "Surplus Government Property, Aircraft, For Sale; List from New York Area," September 6, 1945.

Rust, Kenn C., Fifth Air Force Story, Historical Aviation Album 1973.

Rust, Kenn C., Fifteenth Air Force Story, Historical Aviation Album, 1976.

Rust, Kenn C., Eighth Air Force Story, Historical Aviation Album, 1978.

Schirmer, Col. Frank, "History of 4105th AAF Base Unit 1945-1948," American Aviation Historical Society Journal, Vol 31, No 1, Spring 1986, pp 12-25.

"Scrapped!", Warbird International, July/August 1992. Photos of P-38's in the Philippines.

Serial Numbers Assigned to AAF and DA Aircraft on Approved Contracts From 1939 Program to 15 November 1945, T SBPS-6B, AAF.

Smalley, Lawrence S., Civil Registrations of Surplus Military Aircraft, unpublished manuscript, 1986, 146 pp.

Statistical Study of Registered Civil Aircraft as of November 1, 1947, Civil Aeronautics Administration, Office of Aviation Information.

Statistical Study of U. S. Civil Aircraft as of January 1, 1949, Civil Aeronautics Administration, Office of Aviation Information.

Statistical Study of U. S. Civil Aircraft as of January 1, 1958, Federal Aviation Agency, GPO, Washington, DC.

Statistical Study of U. S. Civil Aircraft as of January 1960, Federal Aviation Agency, GPO, Washington, DC.

Surplus Property Administration, "White Elephants With Wings," GPO 1945.

Surplus Property Board, "Quarterly Report To The Congress," May 28, 1945, 108 pp.

The Liquidation of War Surpluses, Quarterly Progress Report To The Congress by the Surplus Property Administration, Fourth Quarter 1945.

The Official CAA Directory of Certificated Aircraft 1946, Haddaway-Reed Publishing Co., Dallas, TX, 1945.

Thompson, Scott A., Final Cut, Pictorial Histories Publishing Co., 1990.

Thompson, Scott A., "Stillwater," FlyPast, June 2000, pp. 77-80.

United States Civil Aircraft Register June 1, 1963, Federal Aviation Agency, Flight Standards Service, Control Systems Division, GPO ACNo: 20-6. (Lists 110,344 aircraft)

USAF, "History of AF Storage and Withdrawal Program: 1945-52." Incomplete excerpts from a 129-page document.

"US Surplus Aircraft Abroad Sell Slowly," Aviation News, March 12, 1945, pg 15.

Veronico, Nicholas A., Grantham, A. Kevin, and Thompson, Scott, "Military Aircraft Boneyards." MBI Publishing Co., 2000.

Bibliography

WAA, Salable Aircraft Inventory of Sales Storage Depots for Week Ending January 24, 1946.

WAA, Surplus Government Property Special Listing Aircraft, KC List No. 71, March 6, 1946. (Kansas City Region).

WAA, Surplus Government Property Special Listing Aircraft, CG List No. 71, January 15, 1946. (Chicago Region).

WAA, Surplus Government Property Special Listing Aircraft, AT List No. A-193, April 19, 1946. (Atlanta Region).

Ward, Richard and Munday, E.A., USAAF Heavy Bomb Group Markings and Camouflage 1941-1945 Consolidated B-24 Liberator, Osprey Publishing (England), 1972.

War Wings For Peace, Division of Information, War Assetts Administration, Washington, DC, November 1946, 32 pp.

White Elephants With Wings, Surplus Property Administration, GPO, 1945.

Whittle, Dr. John A., "Civil Aircraft Impressed Into USAAF During World War II," Unpublished manuscript, January 1973. 54 pp.

Surplus WWII U.S. Aircraft

AIRCRAFT OWNERS

PARTS FOR YOUR SURPLUS PLANE NOW ARE AVAILABLE NEAR YOU!

Fifty-nine aviation firms have been appointed by the War Assets Administration as agents for the "package" sale of surplus aircraft parts, components, and hardware. They now can supply you with many of the parts that you need to keep flying.

Chosen for their experience and technical "know-how", they are located at strategic points throughout the country to make it convenient for you to fill your needs, and to see what you buy. Many of these are firms with whom you usually deal.

Large quantities of parts have been shipped to WAA agents and new supplies are going out daily.

SEE THEM FOR YOUR NEEDS. THE PRICE IS THE SAME...WHETHER YOU BUY FROM AN AGENT OR DIRECT FROM WAA

If the agents do not yet have what you want, write direct to the Office of Aircraft Disposal, War Assets Administration, Washington 25, D.C. Your order will be given prompt attention.

War Assets Administration Ad

This is a complete list of WAA Authorized Agents for the sale of aircraft parts:

COMPONENTS:

Aircraft Components Corp.
213 King Street
Alexandria, Virginia

Brayton Flying Service, Inc.
Lambert-St. Louis Airport
St. Louis 21, Missouri

Dothan Aviation Company
Municipal Airport
Dothan, Alabama

Florida Aviation Corp.
CAA Station No. 385
Municipal Airport
St. Petersburg, Florida

Grand Central Airport Company
P.O. Box 1315
Glendale 5, California

The Kratz Corporation
Kratz Airport
St. Louis 21, Missouri

Resort Airlines, Inc.
Box 1301 (Southern Pines Airport)
Southern Pines, North Carolina

Southport Aero Service
Rosemount, Minnesota

Thompson Aircraft Products Co. Inc.
23555 Euclid Avenue
2196 Clarkwood Road
Cleveland 17, Ohio

Lynchburg Air Transport & Sales Co.
Preston Glean Airport
Lynchburg, Virginia

Maxwell Associates, Inc.
15 Moore Street
New York 4, New York

New Mexico Aircraft Sales, Inc
West Mesa Airport
P.O. Box 157
Old Albuquerque, New Mexico

Northwestern Aeronautical Corp.
1902 W. Minnehaha
St. Paul 4, Minnesota

Piedmont Aviation, Inc.
Smith Reynolds Airport
Winston-Salem 1, North Carolina

Pyrometer Service Company
228 River Road
North Arlington, New Jersey

Briggs Weaver Machinery Co.
309 N. Market Street
Dallas 2, Texas

Simsbury Flying Service
Simsbury, Connecticut

Spartan Aircraft Company
6900 East Apache
Tulsa, Oklahoma

Toth Aircraft & Accessories Co.
220 Richards Road
Municipal Airport
Kansas City, Missouri

AIRFRAME PARTS:

Douglas Aircraft Company, Inc.
Santa Monica, California

Piper Aircraft Corporation
Lock Haven, Pennsylvania

The Ryan Aeronautical Company
Lindbergh Field
San Diego 12, California

HARDWARE:

Aircraft Steel & Supply Co.
415-425 N. Water Street
Wichita 1, Kansas

Aero Bolt & Screw Co.
1815 Webster Avenue
New York 57, New York

Air Accessories, LTD.
100 East Lancester Street
P.O. Box 1326
Fort Worth 1, Texas

Aircraft Hardware Mfg. Co.
810-812 Edgewater Road
New York 59, New York
also 2344 East 38th Street
Los Angeles, California

Air-Parts, Inc.
723 Sonora Avenue
Glendale 1, California

Clary Multiplier Corp.
1524 90 North Main Street
Los Angeles 12, California

Collins Engineering Company
9050 Washington Blvd.
Culver City, California

Durham Aircraft Service, Inc.
Northern Blvd. at Prince Street
Flushing, New York
also Building No. 3
Douglas Plant
Municipal Airport
Tulsa, Oklahoma

General Aviation Equipment Co.
69 Public Square
Wilkes-Barre, Pennsylvania

Globe Aircraft Corp.
North Side Station
Fort Worth 6, Texas

The S. A. Long Company
232 N. Market Street
Wichita 1, Kansas

Parker Service Agency, Div.
The Parker Appliance Co.
17325 Euclid Avenue
Cleveland 12, Ohio
also 6506 Stanford Avenue
Los Angeles, California

Schuster Electric Co.
321 Sycamore Street
Cincinnati, Ohio

The Stanco Company
1914 Canton Street
Dallas 1, Texas

Snyder Aircraft Corp.
5036 W. 63rd Street
Chicago, Illinois

Supply Division, Inc.
Lambert Airport
Robertson, Missouri

Van Dusen Aircraft Supplies, Inc.
2004 Lyndale Ave., South
Minneapolis 5, Minnesota

The Weatherhead Company
300 East 131st Street
Cleveland 8, Ohio

ENGINE PARTS:

Aviation Activities, Inc.
612 Wholesale Merchants Bldg.
Dallas, Texas

Continental Motors Corp.
c/o Continental Aviation &
Engine Corporation
76 North Getty Street
Muskegon, Michigan

General Wire & Electric Co.
Dodge Building
53 Park Place (Room 409)
New York 7, New York

Pacific Airmotive Corp.
1628 McGee Street
Kansas City 8, Missouri
also 6265 San Fernando Road
Glendale, California

Ranger Aircraft Engines
Division of Fairchild
Engine & Airplane Corp.
Farmingdale, New York

Solar Aircraft Company
2200 Pacific Highway
San Diego 12, California

INSTRUMENTS:

Abrams Instrument Corp.
606 East Shiawassee Street
Lansing 3, Michigan

Eclipse—Pioneer Division
Bendix Aviation Corporation
Teterboro, New Jersey

Jack & Heintz, Inc.
Cleveland 1, Ohio

Kollsman Instrument
Division of Square D Company
80-08 45th Avenue
Elmhurst, New York

Link Aviation Devices, Inc.
Binghamton, New York

Sperry Gyroscope Company, Inc.
Great Neck, Long Island, New York

MISCELLANEOUS:

The G. W. Holmes Company
196-208 East Gay Street
Columbus 15, Ohio

Aero Corporation
Municipal Airport
Atlanta, Georgia

United Aero Service, Inc.
P.O. Box 1028
Delta Air Base
Charlotte, North Carolina

SPECIAL NOTE TO VETERANS: You may use your priority in buying from WAA agents.

WAR ASSETS ADMINISTRATION
WASHINGTON, D. C.

Surplus WWII U.S. Aircraft

HOW ARE YOUR TIRES?

Here is an outstanding opportunity to purchase aircraft tires and tubes at substantially reduced prices. The War Assets Administration has, *in stock*, a wide variety of casings and tubes made for every type of aircraft used by the Armed Forces from small liaison to large cargo planes.

This enormous stock of government-owned surplus represents both unused and used tires and tubes. They are offered in a broad range of sizes, treads and cords for both landing and auxiliary (tail and nose) equipment.

These tires and tubes are suitable for use on airlines, cargo carriers or privately owned planes. Every order will receive careful attention regardless of its size.

These tires and tubes are *low priced* for immediate disposal. Check your needs *now!* Then place your order detailing complete specifications so that price and delivery can be quoted.

If you are located west of the Rockies, address your inquiry to:

WAR ASSETS ADMINISTRATION
155 W. Washington Boulevard
Los Angeles 15, California

If you are located east of the Rockies, address your inquiry to:

WAR ASSETS ADMINISTRATION
National Aircraft Components Sales Center
6200 Riverside Drive
Municipal Airport
Cleveland 32, Ohio

OR

WAR ASSETS ADMINISTRATION
Office of Aircraft Disposal
425 Second Street, N. W.
Washington 25, D. C.

Veterans of World War II:
Veterans may use their priorities in buying these tires and tubes.

War Assets Administration Ad

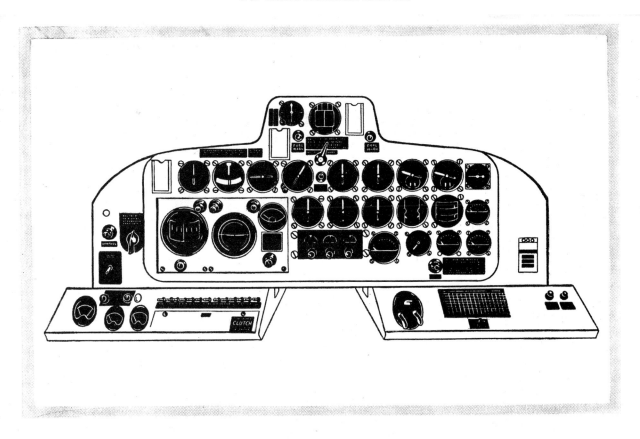

AIRCRAFT INSTRUMENTS

Plane owners, Airline and Fixed Base Operators—if you are interested in purchasing aircraft instruments, the War Assets Administration has a quantity of precision equipment for sale.

This inventory consists of turn and bank indicators, altimeters, gyro horizons, rate of climb indicators, gyro and magnetic compasses and airspeed indicators. There is also a considerable number of engine instruments available.

Designed to attract the prudent buyers, these units are price-scaled according to condition. Many are usable without repairs—others are usable after repairs.

A large supply of type C-3 Link-Trainers in usable and repairable condition are also for sale at attractive prices.

You are invited to detail your requirements so that prices and delivery information may be quoted.

You are urged to contact the WAA Authorized Agent nearest to you. However, if this is not convenient the following WAA offices will be glad to serve you.

If you are located west of the Rockies, address your inquiry to:

WAR ASSETS ADMINISTRATION
155 W. Washington Boulevard
Los Angeles 15, California

If you are located east of the Rockies, address your inquiry to:

WAR ASSETS ADMINISTRATION
National Aircraft Components Sales Center
6200 Riverside Drive, Municipal Airport,
Cleveland 32, Ohio   OR

WAR ASSETS ADMINISTRATION
OFFICE OF AIRCRAFT DISPOSAL
425 Second Street, N. W., Washington 25, D. C.

Veterans of World War II: Veterans may use their priorities in buying these aircraft instruments

AVIATION NEWS • July 8, 1946

Surplus WWII U.S. Aircraft

PROPELLERS

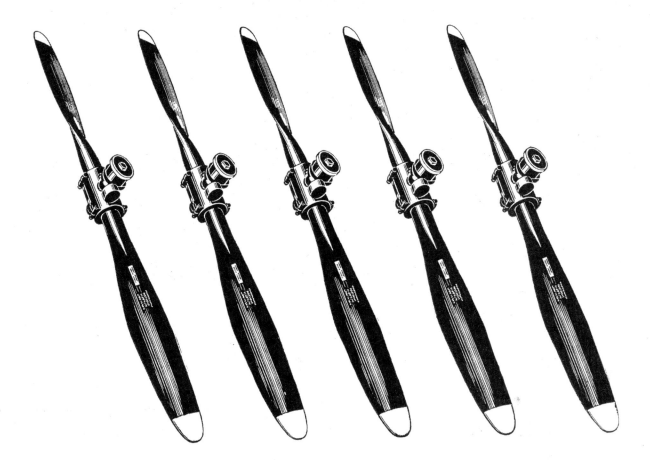

The War Assets Administration has available government-owned surplus aircraft propellers in various models and specifications. These propellers were built by well-known manufacturers of aircraft components to the specifications of the Armed Forces. They are adaptable to planes ranging from light planes to large transports and are eligible for CAA Certification.

Attractively priced for immediate sale, it will pay you to check your requirements *now!*

If you will send your inquiry stating model and detail specifications, prices and delivery information will be forwarded promptly.

You are urged to contact the WAA Authorized Agent nearest to you. However, if this is not convenient the following WAA offices will be glad to serve you.

If you are located west of the Rockies, address your inquiry to:
WAR ASSETS ADMINISTRATION
155 W. Washington Blvd.
Los Angeles 15, California

If you are located east of the Rockies, address your inquiry to:
WAR ASSETS ADMINISTRATION
National Aircraft Components Sales Center
6200 Riverside Drive
Municipal Airport
Cleveland 32, Ohio
OR
WAR ASSETS ADMINISTRATION
Office of Aircraft Disposal
425 Second Street, N. W.
Washington 25, D. C.

Veterans of World War II: Veterans may use their priorities in buying these propellers.

War Assets Administration Ad

MISCELLANEOUS PARTS AND EQUIPMENT

Government-owned surplus in aircraft has produced a quantity of spare parts and equipment both unused and usable with repairs.

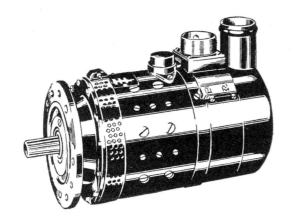

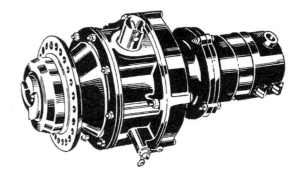

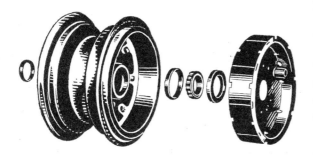

In this inventory are listed such items as: magnetos, motors, generators and other electrical accessories. Various types of wheels and brakes, carburetors and carburetor parts, fuel, oil and hydraulic equipment, miscellaneous engine accessories.

From this store of material you will probably find the things you need to keep you flying. Send your inquiry including specifications on just what you want. Prices and delivery information will be sent to you as speedily as possible.

You are urged to contact the WAA Authorized Agent nearest to you. However, if this is not convenient the following WAA offices will be glad to serve you.

If you are located west of the Rockies, address your inquiry to:	If you are located east of the Rockies, address your inquiry to:
WAR ASSETS ADMINISTRATION	WAR ASSETS ADMINISTRATION
155 W. Washington Boulevard	National Aircraft Components Sales Center
Los Angeles 15, California	6200 Riverside Drive, Municipal Airport
	Cleveland 32, Ohio OR

WAR ASSETS ADMINISTRATION

OFFICE OF AIRCRAFT DISPOSAL
425 Second Street, N. W., Washington 25, D. C.

Veterans of World War II:
Veterans may use their priorities in buying these miscellaneous parts and equipment

Typical WAA & RFC Ads

INDEX

A

AAF Disarmament Division, 16
Aeronca, 124
    L-3, 25, 118
Aircraft Engine Sale, 13
Aircraft Registration Requirement, 11
Aircraft Removal, 11
Aircraft Sales by Bid, 9
Albuquerque, 22
Andrews, Dana, 57
Avro "Anson", 157

B

Barksdale Field, 100
Be Comin Back, 88
Beech,
    AT-10, 15, 23, 29, 52, 128, 135
    AT-11, 5, 145, 151
    C-45, 115, 119
    GB-1, 22, 45, 118
Bell,
    P-39, 14, 23, 52, 57, 64, 161
    P-59, 20, 21, 29
    P-63, 21, 27, 106, 107, 138
Bill of Sale, 116
Bit 'O Lace, 80
Boeing,
    314, 45
    B-17, ix, 9, 14, 15, 16, 17, 21, 29, 52, 71, 75, 80, 86, 89
    B-17G, 11, 13, 19, 83, 86, 87, 88, 89, 128, 130
    B-29, 14, 15, 29, 92, 93
    P2B (B-29), 109
    PB-1 (B-17), 42
    YC-97, 114, 155
Bomb Groups at Kingman, 75
Bowers, Peter M., iii, 96, 111
Brewster, 43
    SB2A, 43
Buchanan Field, x, xii, 24, 115
Budd RB-1, 15, 124

C

Cal-Aero Field, ix, 2, 51, 52
Cessna, 28
    AT-17, 52, 108, 118, 120
    C-78, 52
    JRC-1, 6, 25, 46, 52
    UC-78, 5, 6, 22, 25, 49, 108, 118
Chino Airport, 51
Civil Aeronautics Administration, 3, 5, 117, 127
Civil Aeronautics Board, 33
Civilian Pilot Training Program, 3
Clinton, 19, 20, 22, 39, 49, 52
Clover Field, 162
Concord, x, 3, 5, 25, 26, 32, 33, 34, 45, 46, 48, 110, 112, 113, 115, 119, 120, 124, 126, 148, 149
Consolidated/Convair, 7
    B-24, ix, x, 11, 14, 15, 20, 21, 29, 52, 55, 61, 75, 76, 77, 80, 90, 91, 92, 93, 94, 95, 96, 131
    B-32, 15, 33, 81, 82, 102
    C-87, 33, 91, 95
    LB-30, 91, 128, 131
    P4Y, 109, 114
    PB2Y, 131
    PB4Y-1, 42, 193, 196
    PB4Y, 42, 43, 49, 52, 114
    PBY-5, 146
    PBY-6, 110, 160
    PBY-6A, 42, 110, 154
    RY-1, 18, 33, 141
Constipated Lady, 83
Coutches, Michael, 112
Culver, 140
    PQ-8, 119, 122
    PQ-14, 140
Curtiss, 22
    A-25, 52, 160
    AT-9, 129, 142
    C-46, 21, 27, 29, 35, 36, 52, 62
    O-52, 52, 128, 136
    P-40, xi, 10, 14, 20, 52, 65, 104, 105, 136, 154, 155
    R5C, 42
    SB2C, 41, 49, 58, 154
    SNC-1, 161
    SO3C, 33, 39, 163
Curtiss-Wright Travel Air B-14B, 34

D

Davis, Gladys, 33
Davis-Monthan Air Force Base, 42
DeBona, Joe, 134
Defense Plant Corporation, 3
DeHavilland Mosquito, 156
Douglas, xii
    A-20, 14, 52, 53, 56, 57, 83, 84, 85, 132
    A-24, xi, 14, 52, 64, 158
    A-26, 33, 130
    A-33, 35
    B-18, 26, 145, 150
    B-19, 111
    B-23, ix, 16, 145, 150
    B-26 (A-26), 113
    C-47, x, xii, 5, 6, 10, 13, 15, 17, 27, 52, 118, 119
    C-54, 24, 27, 52, 57, 119, 125
    C-74, 114
    JD (A-26), 42

0, 52, 53, 56, 66, 67
4D, 33, 41, 42, 52, 69, 118
R5D, 113, 119

F

Fairchild,
    AT-21, 32, 52, 163
    C-61, 121
    C-82, 154, 159
    PT-23, 117, 121
    PT-26, x, xii, 17, 34, 118
Fearless F, 87
Federal XPT, 156
Five Grand, 89
Fleetwings,
    YPQ-12A, 12
Foreign Salvage and Sales, 16

G

Gangrene Gertie, 90
General Motors,
    FM-2, 129, 141
    P-75A-1-GC, 13
    TBM, xii, 19, 42, 49, 50, 109, 112, 128, 132
Goeller, Joseph, 119
Goodyear,
    FG-1, 42
Grumman,
    F4F, 47, 49
    F6F, xii, 39, 41, 42, 49, 154, 159
    F8F, 42, 115, 129
    J2F-4, x, 46, 52, 68, 129
    J2F-5, 129, 137
    J2F-6, xii, 32, 41, 52, 129
    J4F-2, 28, 41, 45, 118
    JRF-2, 48, 118
    JRF-6, 119
    OA-14, 118, 122
    TBF, 49, 52, 70, 128
    UC-103, 145, 146

H

Hammer Field, 66, 67
Hi-Blower, 88
Howard, xii
    GH-1, 26
    UC-70, 30, 118
Hughes, Howard, 131, 132

I

Interstate,
    L-6, 119, 125
    TDR-1, 50

K

Kingman, x, xi, xii, xiii, xiv, 8, 9, 15, 19, 20, 21, 22, 41, 52, 71, 74, 75, 81, 86, 91, 92, 96, 98, 102, 104, 105, 106
Kurtz, Frank, 151

L

Latin-American Sales Center, 27
Lear Jr., Bill, 133, 148
Limited Type Certificates, 33, 127, 129
Litchfield Park, 42
Lockheed,
    A-29, 52
    AT-18, 52, 59
    C-69, 36
    F-5, xii, 101, 103, 133
    P-38, xii, 14, 16, 29, 52, 63, 64, 101, 103
    PV-1, 111, 128, 134
    PV-2, 42, 109, 128
    R5O, 45, 52, 70, 118, 122
    R5O-5, 70, 118
    UC-85, ix, 16
    UC-101, 3, 25, 31, 118
Luke Field, 10, 65, 105, 149

M

Maloney, Ed, 52, 112
Mantz, Paul, 3, 22, 31, 50
Martin,
    B-26, 14, 16, 52, 101, 142
    PBM-5, 44, 115, 129, 138
McClellan Field, 112
Metcalf, Charles, 123
Mitchell, John C., 59, 70
My Devotion, 93

N

NAS Alameda, 41, 44, 46
NAS Norfolk, 40, 42, 112
Naval Aircraft Factory,
    N3N, xii, 145, 147, 154, 155
Noorduyn,
    UC-64, 6, 145, 151
    Harvard II, 158
North American,
    A-36, 52, 135
    B-25, viii, 12, 22, 49, 52, 61, 74, 81, 97, 130, 142
    BC-1, 129, 139
    BT-9, xii, 129
    BT-14, 129, 139
    O-47, 52
    P-51, 16, 52, 109, 112, 134, 162
    P-64, 8, 163

SNJ,   xii, 42
T-6,   110, 149
Northrop,
  F-15,   111
  P-61,   4, 29, 52, 70, 136

O

Odom, Bill,   141
Office of Foreign Liquidation,   17
Ontario,   ix, x, xi, xii, 1, 2, 5, 14, 19, 21, 41, 51, 52, 53, 57, 58, 59, 64, 65, 66, PB 67, 68, 69, 70, 112

P

Page, Jane,   161
Perez, Tillie,   x, xii, 33
Piper,
  AE-1,   45, 118
  NE-1,   118, 120
Princess Carol,   92
Public Works Department,   42

R

Reconstruction Finance Corporation,   3, 19, 38, 39, 144, 164
Reed, Boardman C.,   iii, 112, 114, 129
Republic,
  P-47,   xi, 4, 14, 16, 21, 22, 29, 52, 60, 68, 103
  AT-12,   160
Ryan,
  PT-22,   ix, xii, 5, 25, 119, 124

S

Sales of New L-5G Aircraft,   24
Schools and Memorials,   29
Sherman Field,   3, 5, 25, 29, 30, 31, 45, 120, 124
Sikorsky,
  R-4,   131
  R-6,   140
Skelton, Betty,   133
Small Sales at Military Bases,   5
Small Sales Locations,   5
Snowden, H. W.,   22
St. Louis,
  YPT-15,   14, 154, 157
Stearman,
  N2S,   xii, 48, 49, 116, 118
  PT-18,   25, 118
  PT-27,   ix, 118, 123
Steiner, William,   22
Stinson,
  AT-19,   xii, 8, 119, 126
  L-1,   52, 129

L-5,   xii, 15, 16, 119, 126
UC-81,   118
Supermarine "Stranraer,",   147
Surplus Property Act,   3, 7
Surplus Property Board,   3
Surplus War Property Administration,   3

T

Taylorcraft,
  L-2,   25, 118
  TG-6,   52, 145, 149
The Dragon and his Tail,   96
The End of the Program,   35
The Large RFC Fields in the U.S.,   19
The Purple Shaft,   97
Timm,
  N2T,   145, 148
Tinker Field,   58
Trahan, Kenny,   123
Transport Aircraft,   24
Transport Plane Leases,   27
Turner, Glen,   iii, 110, 149

U

Uncle Jim,   90
USS Bairoko CVE-115,   41

V

VE Day (May 8, 1945),   15
VJ Day (September 2, 1945),   15
Vought,
  F4U,   xii, 29, 41, 42, 47, 49
Vought-Sikorsky,
  OS2U-3,   18, 29
Vultee,
  BT-13,   5, 17, 22, 49, 52, 133, 145, 148, 15, 166
  BT-15,   xii, 31
  RA-31C,   20, 28
  SNV-2,   49

W

Waco,   17
  CG-4A,   17
  VKS-7,   5, 45
  YKS-6,   43, 45
Walnut Ridge,   6, 7, 8, 14, 19, 20, 21, 35, 39, 52
War Assets Administration,   x, 3, 5, 12, 22, 35, 109, 152, 200
War Assets Corporation,   3

Cover images:
    Front cover: B-24s at Kingman, Arizona - also shown on page 67.
    Back cover:
        Lockheed F-5G flown by Bill Lear, Jr. - also shown on page 123.
        Grumman J2F-4 "Duck" - also shown on page 42.
Table of Contents image:
        B-24s at Kingman, Arizona - also shown on page 67.